D0467166

Nuclear Weapons Chart

The chart above shows the world's current firepower as opposed to the firepower of World War II. The dot in the center square represents all the firepower of World War II: 3 megatons. The other dots represent the world's present nuclear weaponry which equals 6,000 World War II's or 18,000 megatons. The United States and the Soviets share this firepower with approximately equal destructive capability.

The top left-hand circle enclosing 9 megatons represents the weapons on just one Poseidon submarine. This is equal to the firepower of three World War II's and enough to destroy over 200 of the Soviet's largest cities plus enough to destroy 31 such subs and 10 similar Polaris subs.

The circle in the lower left-hand square enclosing 24 megatons represents one new Trident sub with the firepower of eight Poseidons. Enough to destroy every major city in the northern hemisphere.

The Soviets have similar levels of destructive power.

Just two squares on this chart (300 megatons) represent enough power to destroy all the large- and medium-size cities in the world. (U.S. Senate staff have reviewed this chart and found it a fair representation of the nuclear weapons arsenal.)

THE TRIMTAB
FACTOR

THE TRIMTAB FACTOR

How Business Executives
Can Help Solve the
Nuclear Weapons Crisis

Harold Willens

WILLIAM MORROW AND COMPANY, INC.

New York   1984

Copyright © 1984 by Harold Willens

All rights reserved. No part of this book may be reproduced
or utilized in any form or by any means, electronic or mechanical,
including photocopying, recording or by any information storage
and retrieval system, without permission in writing from the
Publisher. Inquiries should be addressed to William Morrow and
Company, Inc., 105 Madison Avenue, New York, N.Y. 10016.

Library of Congress Cataloging in Publication Data

Willens, Harold.
  The trimtab factor.

  1. Atomic weapons and disarmament.   2. Industry—
Social aspects—United States.   3. Industry and state
—United States.   III. Title.
JX1974.7.W525   1984   327.1'74   83-17202
ISBN 0-688-02661-3

Printed in the United States of America

First Edition

1 2 3 4 5 6 7 8 9 10

BOOK DESIGN BY BERNARD SCHLEIFER

This reaching out to touch the
trimtab of our time is
dedicated to Grace, who has so
graced my life that even during
moments of discouragement or despair,
her love
     . . . remembered such wealth brings
That then I scorn to change my state with Kings.

ACKNOWLEDGMENTS

Mary Earle and Neal Rogin of Mill Valley, California, assisted me immeasurably with the planning, research, and writing of this book. There are no words to convey adequately my appreciation for their help. I wish to express not only my gratitude, but my respect and affection for these two wonderful people who now occupy a special place in my life.

H. W.

Contents

If we do not change our direction,
we are likely to end up where we are headed.

—Ancient Chinese Proverb

THE TRIMTAB
FACTOR

ONE

Case Study of a Good Business Gone Bad

IN A BUSTLING small town nestled at the foot of a large, snow-capped mountain, a young company called USA, Inc. had just weathered a very tough economic period, emerging as a vibrant, resilient, innovative, and energetic organization. It produced a high-quality product in great demand all over town. Pride and morale ran high among its employees and stockholders, and its operating methods were respected and copied by other smaller companies. Yes, for USA, Inc. the future looked bright indeed.

At about this same time, another young company on the other side of town began to make itself known in the marketplace. This company, USSR, Inc., had been taken over by new management. The executive team had some provocative ideas about running the company, but their product was nevertheless shoddy when compared feature for feature with that of USA, Inc. USSR, Inc. sought to overcome this disadvantage by employing very aggressive and less-than-ethical business practices.

There was nothing USSR, Inc. wouldn't do to make inroads into the market dominated by USA, Inc. Their tactics included false advertising, trafficking in rumors and innuendo, industrial espionage, attempted bribes of USA, Inc. employees to reveal valuable production secrets, and even heavy-handed sales techniques to "convince" customers that theirs was the better product. Recently, they had absorbed several smaller companies in entirely ruthless corporate take-overs.

To the officers of USA, Inc. it was obvious that here was no ordinary competitor. Something had to be done. USA's Chief Executive Officer, in an urgent meeting with the board of directors, decided to hire a consultant, a self-proclaimed expert in security.

After studying the situation, the new security specialist concluded that the problem was serious indeed. He predicted that the trend, if left unchecked, could threaten the viability of USA, Inc. He recommended that the company hire additional security guards.

USSR, Inc., interpreting this action as a threat, also added guards and erected a fence around certain sensitive properties. To the security man at USA, Inc., this was an ominous sign. Obviously, the competition had something to hide and posed more of a threat than first assumed. He went back before the CEO and the board of directors.

"I need more money," he told them.

"For what?" they asked.

"We need a stronger guard force. And I want to hire some industrial spies of our own, purely as a defensive measure, you understand. We need to know what the competition is up to."

The USA directors conferred and agreed to give the security expert everything he wanted. After all, he was the expert.

At the next board meeting, the security man was back with a chilling report. "Not only have they matched our increase in guards, plus our fences, but my spies have gotten a copy of their secret business plan. Their policy is to take over all our customers and suppliers! They plan to put us out of business!"

"What do you propose?" one of the board members asked fearfully.

"I think we'd better come up with a plan of our own to put *them* out of business. Of course, I'm going to need a much bigger budget," said the expert, "at least twice the size of my last one. And I want the finest scientific and engineering minds from the Research and Development Division to work with me."

"But," a vice-president protested, "we need those resources to run our business."

The security man leaned across the table. "Look," he said dramatically, "if I don't get the resources I need, you won't have a business!" Panicked, the board gave him everything he wanted, including a permanent position as a member of the board.

A few weeks later, the security chief called the board together. "Those boys you sent me from R & D are brilliant," he began. "Working together, we have come up with an almost foolproof way of keeping our competition from expanding any further."

"What is it?" the board members asked.

"You know that land we own up on the mountain? Well, we have figured out a way to rig an explosive charge up there so if we set it off, an avalanche will bury USSR, Inc.—headquarters, factory, offices, and all!"

"How could that possibly be of benefit to our company?" an officer inquired.

"It's simple," the security chief replied. "The threat that we can put them out of business will keep USSR, Inc. from doing anything that would be against our interests. If they're afraid we'll bury them, they'll think twice about stepping out of line."

"But isn't that a little drastic?" a vice-president asked.

"You still don't seem to understand," the security chief

responded. "Remember the last time another company tried to take over our territory? How despicable they turned out to be, how evil?" The board members nodded their heads in unison. "Remember how we held off, letting them get more and more entrenched? And what a mistake it turned out to be for us not to take that threat seriously?"

"Of course we do," they answered in one voice. "We almost lost the company."

"Well," said the security chief, slamming his fist on the table, "USSR, Inc. is *WORSE!*"

The board members fell back in their chairs, aghast. The Chief Executive Officer was the first to speak.

"Well, it looks like we have no choice. I recommend that we give him what he needs." Reluctantly, the board agreed, and it was done.

A few weeks later, they learned to their horror that their competitor had done the very same thing. USSR, Inc. had purchased its own land up on the mountain and was rigging it with explosive devices capable of causing an avalanche that would bury USA, Inc. In a special session, the board once again listened intently to the security chief's words.

"We simply cannot allow them to catch up to us like this. We must stay ahead at all costs! The entire future of our company, our way of doing business, is at stake. This is an emergency!"

With a massive infusion of personnel and resources, the security office grew to become the enormous Security Division, the largest single component of USA, Inc. During this period, the operating policy of USA, Inc. shifted dramatically. No longer did USA, Inc. lead the way into new markets with innovative products and production techniques. Instead, the USA management formulated a policy based on reacting to whatever USSR, Inc. was doing. The policy could be summarized in these terms: "Whatever they do, we'll do the opposite . . . and whatever they are for, we are against." The company abandoned its former positive, forward-looking, optimistic operating policy based on making the best product at the lowest price. USA, Inc. was now committed to a negative, pessimistic, and reactive approach called "knock the competition."

The most important single aspect of their work became something they called "corporate security." Anyone who questioned company policy was sternly castigated. "Do you want to endanger corporate security? Whose side are you on, anyway?"

Before long, half of the company's most valuable resource, its brightest technical and managerial minds, were working solely on security projects. Forty percent of USA, Inc.'s entire operating budget, already in the red, was reserved for security-related expenditures. Research that had once been directed toward developing new and better products was now applied to developing more and more elaborate and expensive security devices. USA, Inc. even opened a profitable little side business supplying its sophisticated security devices to smaller, noncompetitive, "friendly" companies. Still, USSR, Inc. kept pace, and even seemed to make some inroads into the market.

Over a period of years, the two companies matched each other's self-protective measures stride for stride, leapfrogging from one complex and dangerous new security system to the next, USA, Inc. trying to stay ahead, USSR, Inc. trying to keep up. Both companies were now pouring massive amounts of money and talent into developing the ultimate, once-and-for-all overwhelming threat against the other.

Soon the mountain was so laden with highly sophisticated, supersensitive, hair-trigger explosives that no one could go near it. In fact, there were now so many explosives that if only a small portion were to go off, even accidentally, it would trigger an enormous avalanche that would bury not only the two companies, but the entire town as well.

The public relations departments of both competitors were busy keeping the townspeople from becoming alarmed. This was not as difficult as it seemed. Since the danger had built up so slowly over the years, people scarcely noticed it. It seemed to them that the companies had always had explosives on the mountain—they were a fact of life. Anyway, none of them had gone off yet.

Through an astonishing run of good luck, the two competitors continued on for years without setting off an avalanche. USA, Inc.'s board concluded that its policy must be working. But eventually, the effects of the diversion of the company's resources to security began to show themselves. The quality of the USA, Inc. product began to slip badly, and so did sales. As demand went down, profits plunged, and so did the morale of employees and shareholders. Other smaller companies, which were spending only a tiny fraction of their resources on security, were able to turn out better products at lower prices and to make serious inroads into markets formerly dominated by USA, Inc. Before long, assembly lines had to be shut down and workers laid off. The company's physical plant was deteriorating and there wasn't enough money left in the budget to pay for maintenance and repairs. Feelings of disillusionment and despair now prevailed.

But it was not just USA, Inc. employees who were affected. USSR, Inc. was also in trouble, and as a result, the entire town began to suffer. Its once-thriving economy was stagnating, there being little flow of capital or products except for security devices. The town council had to cut back on police, fire, health, and educational services. The townspeople grew hungrier and angrier. People became so desperate they would do anything for food or money. Soon the streets were unsafe both day and night; nice neighborhoods turned into slums, some parts became shantytowns, and no one, not even executives of the two big corporations, was safe anymore.

Things got so bad that at the annual meeting of USA, Inc. shareholders, people demanded an explanation. The CEO and the board gave them several. "Low worker motivation," they said. "Inflation," they said. "Unfair competition," they said. "Not enough security," they said. They proposed to rectify the situation by cutting employees' benefits such as health plans and retirement so there would be more money available for security.

Unwilling to come to grips with the immense peril they had created for themselves and everyone in the town, USA, Inc. continued its slide down a path that was leading slowly and inexorably toward bankruptcy . . . or worse, toward the ultimate avalanche.

Global war has become a Frankenstein to destroy both sides. No longer is it a weapon of adventure—the shortcut to international power. If you lose, you are annihilated. If you win, you stand only to lose. No longer does it possess even the chance of the winner of a duel. It contains only the germs of double suicide.

—GENERAL DOUGLAS MACARTHUR

Even the ingenuity of our scientists may be unable to save us from the consequences of a single rash act or a lone reckless hand upon the switch of an uninterceptible missile. Missiles will bring antimissiles, and antimissiles will bring anti-antimissiles. I do not understand why we do not make greater, more imaginative use of reason and intelligence in seeking an accord and compromise that will make it possible for mankind to control the atom and banish it as an instrument of war.

—GENERAL OMAR BRADLEY

Just two U.S. Poseidon submarines can destroy all the 200 major Soviet cities.

Just two Soviet Delta III submarines can destroy the 200 major U.S. cities.

—CAPTAIN JAMES T. BUSH (USN Ret.) Former Commanding Officer, Polaris Submarine

21

TWO

The Trimtab Factor

As a businessman, I know that the rigors of the marketplace demand pragmatic, tough-minded thinking. In the world of business, unexamined assumptions, justifications, and self-deception can become prescriptions for bankruptcy. Successful executives, managers, and entrepreneurs must be objective, open-minded, and flexible. They must know when it is time to cut losses and move in a new direction. These are precisely the qualities that need to be brought to bear on the nuclear weapons crisis.

Members of the business community also possess inordinate power and influence in our society. My years of political involvement have proved to me that policymakers are more receptive and responsive to business than to any other single constituency.

This combination of pragmatism and political influence is unique to the business sector. That is why I believe business leadership is the key to the way out of the nuclear weapons dilemma.

For more than twenty years, I have searched for ways to convey with sufficient force, intensity, and urgency the unparalleled significance of the change that took place with the first atomic explosion. We have entered an era in which a few men can, within minutes, destroy thousands of cities, hundreds of millions of people, centuries of human civilization, and quite possibly all life on earth.

As a Marine intelligence officer trained to speak Japanese, I was witness to what was left of Hiroshima and Nagasaki in the early days of the American occupation of Japan. In long letters to my wife I attempted to describe the unbelievable destruction caused in each city by a single "new bomb." I told her how I stood where buildings had once stood—buildings that the blast had transformed into powder I could sift through my fingers. Not mounds of rubble, but piles of powder. I wrote that I stood in places where people had simply evaporated—"disappeared by suddenly becoming nothing," in the words of one survivor. And more than once, I stressed my fervent wish that the leaders of nations who would ever have this device of awesome destruction could see and hear what I was seeing and hearing in Hiroshima and Nagasaki.

The impact of that experience faded as I returned to civilian life, devoting myself entirely to family and business matters. By 1960 the success of a textile-related company I had created with a close friend and real-estate investments I had made gave me considerable economic independence. The free-enterprise system had made it possible for me to achieve an economic level I could hardly have dreamed possible during my childhood of deep poverty. I had special reason, then, to feel great reverence for the system that enriched my life in ways I could never hope to repay.

But gradually, there grew within me the feeling that I must try to give something back to the country that had given me the great gift of the good life. As the saying goes: Now that I had done well, I wanted to do good. The question became: How?

While I was exploring various possibilities, I attended a seminar at the Center for the Study of Democratic Institutions in Santa Barbara, California. The issue under discussion was the Soviet-American nuclear arms race. The gist of the several-day dialogue came down to this: The real problems of our shrinking world were growing more pressing and perilous. Yet the United States and the Soviet Union—the two nations with the greatest stake in finding solutions to those problems—were instead diverting their attention and resources to a runaway nuclear arms race neither side could ever win. The cost and danger could only escalate, and the example being set by the two superpowers could only result in other nations deciding to join the nuclear weapons club. Thus, one could foresee a world filled with nuclear armed nations, and terrorists as well. How could the U.S. and the U.S.S.R. equate that kind of world with their own national security?

The discussion ignited in me the memory of what I had witnessed in Japan in 1945 and jolted me into a decision that would alter the course of my life. Increasingly during the years following, the focus of my attention became, and has remained, the nuclear arms race—the one potentially terminal problem of our time.

We have adjusted neither our thinking, our actions, nor our language to the realities of the nuclear age. In the era of thermonuclear technology, the terms "war" and "weapons" have become dangerously inaccurate and misleading. Is something that can incinerate a city in seconds a "weapon"? Are we "armed" if we are able to blow up an entire nation in a matter of minutes? Do we call it a "war" if two great countries can devastate each other and destroy the life-protecting ecosphere of our planet?

Nuclear weapons could be more accurately described as "devices of ultimate annihilation," and nuclear war deserves its own new word, *omnicide*: "the killing of everything." The term nuclear holocaust approaches accuracy, the word holocaust meaning "great and total destruction of life, especially by fire." Perhaps if we actually used these terms, we would begin to recognize the profound change that has occurred, the enormity of its consequences, and the grave danger we face as nuclear devices multiply throughout the world.

In the early days of the nuclear age, Albert Einstein warned the people of the world and their governments of "the unprecedented disaster which they are absolutely certain to bring on themselves unless there is a fundamental change in their attitudes toward one another as well as in their concept of the future. The unleashed power of the atom," Einstein went on to say, "has changed everything except our way of thinking, and thus we drift toward unparalleled catastrophe."

Living in the new reality of the nuclear age, we nevertheless cling to the perceptions and policies of the prenuclear world, a world where more weapons *did* make us safer, where warfare *could* achieve political ends. What will it take for us to change our way of thinking?

I believe the business community has a unique role to play in bringing about the transformation in consciousness that must occur if we are to survive. Business is the most flexible and change-oriented segment of our society. Constant interaction with marketplace realities makes it necessary for executives, managers, and entrepreneurs to reassess policies at regular intervals, evaluating them in terms of the costs, benefits, and risks involved. Successful business leaders must be ready to abandon unworkable policies and adopt new strategies to meet new challenges. This realistic and pragmatic approach must now be applied to our nation's nuclear weapons policy. The capabilities and characteristics that make for success in the competitive marketplace are precisely those that can break the momentum of the nuclear arms race.

Over nearly forty years, the steady acceleration of the Soviet–American nuclear weapons race has given it a force and momentum that seem impossible to stop or change. Given the ideological, technological, and bureaucratic inertia involved in our government's nuclear weapons policy, many Americans have come to believe that while the arms race is unfortunate, it is a necessary fact of life. But the continual accumulation of devices of mass destruction is not inevitable. We can assure our national security without continually adding to our nuclear arsenal. We can slow, stop, and gradually reverse the nuclear arms race.

In accomplishing this enormous task, the leverage of the business community can be a critical factor. Now, more than at any time in our history, we need to hear the voice of business, a voice that can make itself heard and heeded. Business leadership can provide what renowned architect, inventor, and philosopher R. Buckminster Fuller called the "trimtab" factor.

On airplane wings, and on the keels of racing yachts, trimtabs are small adjustable flaps that assist in balancing and steadying the motion of the craft. The principle of the trimtab also applies to a ship's rudder. In explaining the trimtab factor, Buckminster Fuller used the image of a large oceangoing ship traveling at high speed through the water. The mass and momentum of such a vessel are enormous, and great force is required to turn its rudder and change the ship's direction. In the past, some large ships had, at the trailing edge of the main rudder, another tiny rudder—the trimtab. By exerting a small amount of pressure, one person could easily turn the trimtab. The trimtab then turned the rudder, and the rudder turned the ship. Thus, the trimtab factor demonstrates how the precise application of a small amount of leverage can produce a powerful effect.

Business is the trimtab of America, a sector of society that possesses inordinate power to influence the direction of our national enterprise. Our ship of state is taking us into very dangerous waters. Business leadership can be the trimtab that will change our direction before it is too late.

The Pentagon defends MIRV as necessary to insure penetration of a heavy ABM defense, which the Soviets *might* build. Pentagon Research Chief John Foster has testified there is no evidence the Soviets have started such a system and that if they do, it will take five years to build it. In other words, the Pentagon is deploying this weapon at least four years in advance of the Soviet deployment it reportedly is a reaction to. If that sounds as fishy to Soviet diplomats as it does to us . . . their generals would inevitably want to press harder with their own multiple warhead testing.

—*The Wall Street Journal*
1969 editorial

In 1969 and 1970 I wish we had thought through the implications of a MIRV'ed world.

—**HENRY KISSINGER**
December 1974

THREE

Origins of a
Bad Business Policy

OUR CASE STUDY of a good business gone bad (see Chapter
One) is more than a metaphor. The United States is not
merely like a business. America *is* business—a distinct entity
whose marketplace is the entire world, and whose health is
measured in terms of economic vitality and well-being. Any
objective observer cannot fail to conclude that USA, Inc. faces
an unprecedented crisis. Unless there is a change in the company's operating policy, it could lose everything in a final
bankruptcy from which there would be no recovery.

It is obvious that the impetus for change will not come
from within the management of USA, Inc. Commitment to a
policy based on outdated beliefs and unquestioned assumptions blinds them to the consequences of their present course.
The only thing that could alter their policy—short of a catastrophe—would be a powerful outside influence, someone
who could help steer the company in a new direction.

In order to achieve results, this consultant would need to
have considerable expertise and a track record of success. To
be effective, the consultant would also have to be someone
who commands influence, whose opinions and judgments are
respected by management. These characteristics are embod-
ied in the most influential segment of American society, the
business community.

You could be the consultant who can advise USA, Inc. on how to chart a new course. As a business person, your experience, your approach to problem analysis, and your potential for political persuasiveness all place you in a unique position to influence the course of the American enterprise at this critical time in its history.

In your role as consultant, this book is meant to serve as a briefing. It will provide background on the scope and dimension of the problem: information on the origin and history of the nuclear weapons competition; an evaluation of the cost and consequences of America's present nuclear policies; and a realistic assessment of the threat posed by our major competitor, the Soviet Union.

The briefing then presents an alternative to the nuclear arms race—a course that could stabilize the highly volatile world situation, reduce the appeal of communism, and release enormous resources that could help initiate an economic renaissance in many parts of the world. We cannot set out on such a course, however, while pursuing an ever-accelerating nuclear arms race. Millions of concerned citizens of the world are hopeful the United States can lead the way out of the current nuclear impasse.

But before we can examine the way out, we must understand the forces, events, and attitudes that have brought us to our present crisis. Or to put it in the model of our case study, how did a company with such a good product and brilliant future get itself into such a dangerous and self-defeating predicament?

From birth, the United States was a highly experimental enterprise, perhaps the greatest experiment in human history. Here was a great land rich in natural resources, its population representative of all the peoples of the world. It was a nation created to discover the answer to a question nèver before asked in human history: Given freedom and the opportunity to determine their own destiny, what could human beings accomplish?

For more than a century and a half, through wars, depressions, and the remarkable transformation from an agricultural to an industrial society, it was established that the experiment could work—that there could be a social order in which political and economic freedom could enable people to live and work together to achieve their highest potentialities. It was far from a perfect society, but its problems were seen as opportunities, and Americans struggled to make "life, liberty, and the pursuit of happiness" reality rather than rhetoric.

Then, in 1941, the nation put aside its purely American pursuits and reluctantly took up weapons to defend itself and the free world from the very real threat of Nazi Germany. The people of the United States did so with the understanding and the promise that when it was all over, they would again pick up the great American experiment where they had left it and resume the journey. But that never happened. America went to war in 1941 and never came back.

For soon after the war, a nation at the height of its power, the unquestioned leader of the industrial world, found its national pride turning to national panic. Interpreting the Soviet takeover of Eastern Europe as proof of Russia's aggressive aims and intention to conquer the world, our policymakers assumed communism to be an even greater danger than Nazi Germany. It was, we were told, a threat of such dimension and importance that we must without question subordinate and even sacrifice our most important national goals in order to protect ourselves and the world against it. Transferring our fear and hatred of the Nazis to the Soviet Union, we changed the name of the enemy and the name of the war and continued the conflict. Thus, without missing a beat, we marched from the temporary emergency of World War II into the permanent policy known as the Cold War.

America's national aims, whatever they had been or were

going to be, suddenly took a backseat to our new number-one priority: stopping the Russians. We called it "containment," but what it really represented was a complete shift in the nature, direction, and purpose of the American enterprise.

Thus, U.S. foreign policy in the years immediately following World War II became the mirror image of Soviet foreign policy. Whatever the Russians did, we did the opposite. Any nation they opposed, we supported, no matter how oppressive the regime. Rather than expanding upon the compassion, statesmanship, and enlightened self-interest of programs like the Marshall Plan, we became obsessed with arming ourselves and our allies to meet the Communist threat.

Our domestic policies as well revolved around the Soviet Union: No political candidate could be elected without professing hatred for the Russians, and no aspect of foreign policy or foreign aid could be enacted unless it was thought that the Russians would oppose it. Most important was the unwritten law that Americans remain entirely ignorant of Soviet communism. Teachers were fired for teaching about it; people lost their jobs for reading about it.

As a result, the competing economic and political system about which we should have known the most, we knew the least, and our ignorance only served to fuel our fears. Imagine how long a successful business venture would continue to prosper if it ignored the basic principle "know the competition" and deliberately sought to remain ignorant of the plans, policies, and capabilities of its major competitor!

America had convinced itself that it had no choice but to sacrifice its own best interests in order to resist the purposes of a rival political system. In short, an irrational and debilitating fear of the Russians—"Russophobia"—became an obsession that made the people of the most powerful nation on earth feel threatened, vulnerable, and afraid.

Caught in the grip of Russophobia, America succumbed to yet another malady, "militaritis"—an excessive dependence on military power and military solutions. Rather than responding to the challenge of the changing world order in political and economic ways, the United States came to rely primarily on its military power. Every crisis and every opportunity came to be viewed in military terms. Whatever the problem, the solution was military. Whatever the question, the answer was military. Whatever the threat, the response was military.

The American people hardly seemed to notice this profound change, or if they did, believed it to be necessary given the aggressive threat of world communism. This perception was reinforced by the semantic military coup that occurred in 1947 when the War Department was renamed the Department of Defense. Suddenly, the very same activities that were once considered acts of war were perceived as acts of national defense. Indeed, all of our military actions, including the containment of communism in other parts of the world, became issues of defense. Instead of a war budget or a military budget or a weapons budget, we had a defense budget. How could upstanding citizens criticize our defense policies or question defense spending? Could a legislator who wanted to stay in office afford to speak out or vote against our national defense?

National defense became the one problem at which the U.S. Congress seemed intent on throwing money. Over the years, our elected representatives fell into the pattern of rubber-stamping Pentagon budget requests with virtually no scrutiny of aims and strategies. Increasingly higher sums were allocated with only perfunctory debate, and the nation's taxpayers seemed more than willing to foot the bill.

Writing in 1964, Senator J. William Fulbright, then chairman of the Senate Foreign Relations Committee, stated:

Of all the changes in America's life wrought by the cold war, the most important by far, in my opinion, has been

35

the mass diversion of energy and resources to the conduct of a costly and interminable struggle for world power. We have been compelled, or felt ourselves compelled, to reverse the traditional order of our national priorities, relegating individual and community life to places on the scale below the enormously expensive military and space activities that constitute our program of national security. . . . The truly astonishing thing about the uncritical support which the American people and their representatives give the military establishment is the apparent enthusiasm with which the sacrifice of personal and community interests are made.

America's drift into an increasingly militarized society was viewed with alarm by President Eisenhower, a military man himself, who warned of "the acquisition of unwarranted influence, whether sought or unsought, by the military-industrial complex." For, as he went on to say, "the potential for the disastrous rise of misplaced power exists and will persist." Yet over nearly four decades, militaritis, like Russophobia, continued to form the basis of our national security policy.

Perhaps it was the bitter lesson we learned from having been insufficiently prepared for World War II that caused many Americans to perceive the Soviet threat as identical to the Nazi threat, to be dealt with only by military means. Perhaps it was our ignorance of the profound implications of having released the nuclear genie from its bottle that caused us to misunderstand the new consequences of military competition. Whatever the reason, rather than apply ourselves to finding political solutions for the new and complex problems of the postwar nuclear world, we embraced instead the age-old patterns of military rivalry. America opted for being stronger rather than being smarter, using bombs rather than brains to meet the challenges of a changing world and a competitive ideology.

In our preoccupation with military responses, we over-looked the economic and political aspects of life in which the American free-enterprise system uniquely excels. We chose instead to compete with the Soviets in the one arena in which they were capable of keeping up—*military might*.

In the past three decades, the United States has paid dearly for its excessive dependence on military solutions to nonmilitary problems—not merely in terms of the trillions of dollars spent, but also in lives lost defending interests that could better be protected in other ways. The world community—particularly the developing nations—has also paid the price of superpower militarism, finding little left over for economic development after the bill for world military expenditures is paid. While the superpowers spend billions on armaments, one quarter of humanity starves. With the Third World mired in poverty, the enormous market potential of the developing countries remains untapped by the developed nations whose industrial capacity is severely underutilized.

There is also a moral tragedy that stems from our susceptibility to Russophobia and militaritis. Interpreting every national revolution as Communist-inspired or potentially Communist-oriented, we chose to align ourselves with the forces of the *status quo*, no matter how unpopular or oppressive. Our support was given to brutal dictators as long as they declared themselves to be anti-Communist. Revolution, then, became our enemy—a supreme historic irony, given our own revolutionary origins. Rather than inspiring the world with the functional model of a free-enterprise democracy, we instead assumed the role of world policeman. We chose to expand and maintain our position not through commerce and compassion, but through conflict and coercion.

This choice represented a fundamental failure on our part. We had an unprecedented opportunity to make the results of our own national experiment—the fruits of our own revolution—available to the developing countries of the world. We could have offered them a better standard of living and served as a model of democracy and freedom. We could have offered an authentic alternative to the grim choices between authoritarianism of the right and totalitarianism of the left, but we failed to seize the initiative or even grasp the meaning of the fateful decisions we were making.

But the highest price of a purely militaristic response to the Communist challenge is yet to be paid, a deferred debt that can be postponed for only so long, and could come due at any moment: nuclear annihilation. In pursuing a policy of military confrontation with the Soviet Union, we have chosen a form of competition in which there can be no winner and weapons that, if used, would destroy us both. We have locked ourselves into a nuclear weapons race that has come to have a life of its own.

As a consultant to our national enterprise, it is appropriate that you scrutinize the origin, history, and potential consequences of a costly and perilous policy. What are the motivations for the arms race? What do we hope to achieve? Can the nuclear arms race be won? Or is it, as one observer has stated, the "race to oblivion"?

If a great number of countries come to have an arsenal of nuclear weapons, then I am glad that I am not a young man and I am sorry for my grandchildren.

—DAVID LILIENTHAL
First Chairman
U.S. Atomic Energy
Commission
1976

We will eat leaves and grass, even go hungry, but we will have to get one [a bomb] of our own.

—ALI BHUTTO
Premier, Pakistan
1974

Let us not be told especially about de-nuclearizing Africa when South Africa already has a nuclear arsenal. . . . The duty of the Africans that can is to resolutely embark on the nuclear path.

—EDEM KODJO
Secretary General
Organization of Africa
Unity
June 9, 1983

The nation which indulges toward another an habitual hatred, or an habitual fondness, is in some degree a slave. It is a slave to its animosity or to its affection, either of which is sufficient to lead it astray from its duty and its interest.

—GEORGE WASHINGTON
Farewell Address to the
People of the United States
1796

FOUR

A Competition No One Can Win

ON JULY 16, 1945, the first nuclear explosion turned sand into glass in the New Mexico desert. Twenty-one days later, the world learned the stunning news that with a single new bomb the United States had leveled an entire Japanese city. Three days after that another city was destroyed. Obscured by the relief that at last World War II had ended was the faint recognition that something else—perhaps something terrible— had begun.

For the next four years the United States enjoyed the preeminent position of being the world's only nuclear power. The explosion by the Soviet Union of its first atomic bomb in 1949 ended that short-lived era, and sounded the starting gun for a new competition, the headlong race to produce and deploy devices of mass destruction.

In early years of the competition, when the United States possessed undisputed superiority in nuclear weapons, American policy was based on the concept of massive retaliation: the threat that any aggressive move against American interests by the Soviet Union could provoke a massive attack on Russian population centers and result in the destruction of the Soviet economy and millions of Russian citizens.

This policy, coupled with U.S. superiority, was an impor-

41

tant factor during the Cuban Missile Crisis, when President Kennedy was able to force Soviet Premier Khrushchev to back down and remove Russian missiles from Cuba. Unfortunately, this confrontation had the effect of increasing Soviet determination that they would never again be thwarted because of nuclear inferiority. It was at this time that the U.S.S.R. began its own nuclear weapons buildup in earnest, while the U.S. redoubled its efforts to maintain superiority. The arms race shifted into a higher gear, fueled by the pre-nuclear notion that "more is better."

By the late 1960's, the Russians had amassed an awesome nuclear arsenal of their own, ushering in the age of deterrence, a strategy based on the idea that if either side can respond to an attack with a devastating counterattack, the aggressor would be deterred for fear of his own destruction. This policy was given the acronym MAD, for Mutual Assured Destruction.

Some considered MAD to be a sensible approach to an extremely difficult situation. After all, if each side possessed enough destructive power to prevent its adversary from attacking, both sides would achieve a relatively permanent, if dangerous, stability. But even achieving a delicate balance of terror did not deter the continued acceleration of the arms race. Neither the Russians nor the Americans were willing to answer—or even ask—the question: How much deterrence is enough?

Assuming that one hundred hydrogen bombs dropped on one hundred cities in either country would wipe out a quarter of the population and destroy up to half of the industrial base, it follows that for an effective deterrent, each country would need fewer than one thousand nuclear devices (assuming that only one in ten bombs would hit its target). Robert McNamara, Secretary of Defense in the 1960's, concluded that the United States would need only about four hundred one-megaton bombs to maintain an adequate deterrent force against the Soviet Union. But such a conclusion had little impact on the arms race, which McNamara described as having a "mad momentum" of its own.

In the 1970's, despite the apparent thaw in the Cold War known as detente and the SALT I agreement (the Strategic Arms Limitation Treaty, which did not limit nuclear weapons but set a slower pace for their development), the competition continued unabated. American technological and economic superiority enabled the U.S. to stay ahead, but any lead was never permanent. No matter what technological advantage the U.S. achieved—whether in nuclear weapons or delivery systems—within a few years, the Soviet Union would catch up. Each time, this would cause a series of alarms to echo through the halls of government that the United States might be losing its superior edge. Each of these occasions would generate a vigorous campaign to enlist American taxpayers' support for yet another generation of weapons systems.

America's traumas of the 1970's—Vietnam, Watergate, the energy crisis, inflation, unemployment, Iran, and Afghanistan—seemed to shake the nation's faith in itself and its military power. This self-doubt extended itself into worries about the effectiveness of our nuclear deterrent. By the end of the decade, what was interpreted by some as a massive Soviet military buildup led to claims that the U.S. was actually falling behind. These fears of nuclear inferiority generated opposition to SALT II, the treaty negotiated in a second round of strategic-arms-limitation talks. After the Soviet invasion of Afghanistan in December of 1979, President Carter withdrew SALT II from Senate consideration. America's alleged inferiority was a major issue in the 1980 presidential campaign, and Ronald Reagan interpreted his victory as a mandate for an intensive effort to "reestablish American superiority."

In 1981, the Reagan administration called for a $1.6-

trillion military budget over five years. At the same time, both the weapons and the rhetoric of the nuclear arms race took on a new and ominous dimension. In a distinct departure from the defensive posture of deterrence, individuals in the Pentagon and in the administration were talking openly about waging "limited nuclear war" with "surgical first strikes" and tactical nuclear weapons, as well as scenarios for fighting and winning an all-out nuclear war. The administration's fiscal 1983 budget statement proclaimed—for the first time in the history of the arms race—that "U.S. defense policies ensure our preparedness to respond to and, if necessary, successfully fight either a conventional or nuclear war."

Unprecedented statements about the survivability of nuclear war, as well as plans for new weapons systems that could provide a first-strike option, generated public uncertainty as to whether American strategy was to deter nuclear war or to "prevail" (a euphemism for "win") in a protracted nuclear war. For the first time since a public outcry forced an end to atmospheric testing of nuclear weapons in 1963, there emerged in America and Europe a groundswell of opposition to nuclear armaments and massive support for a freeze on the testing, production, and deployment of nuclear weapons by both the U.S. and the U.S.S.R.

Despite the public reaction, the Reagan administration initiated the largest peacetime military buildup in American history. It did, however, respond by initiating a new round of U.S.–Soviet negotiations called START (Strategic Arms Reductions Talks), which began in 1982. But the prospects for arms control, much less reductions, seemed grim as both sides continued to claim they should not have to reduce because the other was ahead.

Who is winning the arms race? As of 1983, most experts were in agreement that the strategic forces of the United States and the Soviet Union possessed equivalent capability to destroy the other no matter who attacked first. The only difference is that more of the Soviet force is carried on land-based missiles and more of the U.S. force on long-range bombers and missile-firing submarines.

But while the issue of superiority or inferiority remains the perennial focus of debate, the real question is: *What does it matter?* Or as former Secretary of State Henry Kissinger put it in 1974, "What in the name of God is strategic 'superiority'? What is the significance of it, politically, militarily, operationally, at these levels? What do you do with it?"

The United States has about thirty thousand nuclear weapons of all types and the Soviet Union has about twenty thousand (according to 1983 estimates). At that level, the U.S. could destroy every Russian city of over one hundred thousand people *thirty-five* times, and the Soviets could destroy every city of more than one hundred thousand Americans *twenty-seven* times. The arsenals of the adversaries have become so redundant that nuclear strategists on both sides would run out of worthwhile targets to hit long before they ran out of bombs.

We must keep reminding ourselves that nuclear devices are not merely larger, more destructive versions of conventional weapons. The nuclear devices on just one of America's thirty-four strategic missile submarines could generate three times the explosive power detonated in Europe and the Pacific during all of World War II. Admiral Noel Gayler (Ret.), former director of the National Security Agency and at one time a Commander of U.S. Forces in the Pacific, has stated, "What Americans do not understand is that there is no sensible military use for any of the three categories of nuclear weapons—strategic, theater, or tactical."

Supposedly, theater or tactical weapons would prevent a limited confrontation from becoming an all-out nuclear war. But who can possibly count on a nice tit-for-tat strategy in the thermonuclear heat of battle? The more likely scenario is that the losing side would escalate to bigger weaponry before giving up. Very few people in the scientific or military establishments give credence to the concept of limited nuclear war. Common sense alone should have us assume that any nuclear exchange would mean full-scale nuclear war.

Even if we manage, somehow, to avoid a nuclear conflagration between the United States and the Soviet Union, we must recognize that there are other possible, even increasingly probable, paths to nuclear war. As weapon is piled upon weapon, the danger of a nuclear war occurring by accident or miscalculation becomes more and more likely.

Accidents involving nuclear weapons have become common enough that the Pentagon has a code name for them: "Broken Arrows." Thirty-two of these mishaps have been well publicized. Many more remain unknown to the general public.

On hundreds of occasions, U.S. nuclear-warning-system computers have mistakenly indicated Soviet attacks, and many of these warnings have been serious enough to require response decisions. One such false alarm was triggered by the rising of the moon; another by the failure of a forty-six-cent computer part; yet another by the inadvertent feeding of a war-game tape into the computer. Recent tests by the Pentagon of its computer nerve center, the Worldwide Military Command and Control System, showed that overall, the computers failed 62 percent of the time. Similar accidents have probably occurred in the Soviet Union with at least equal frequency.

In addition, there have been a number of serious mishaps involving our own weapons. In Damascus, Arkansas, in 1980, a Titan II missile exploded when a wrench, dropped accidentally by a workman, punctured the missile and ignited its fuel, hurling a nine-megaton warhead a distance of two hundred yards. There have been twenty-seven accidents involving air-planes carrying nuclear weapons. In 1961, a B-52 carrying two nuclear weapons crashed in California, and in the same year, another B-52 jettisoned a twenty-four-megaton bomb in North Carolina. When found, all but one of the bomb's six interlocking safety devices had been triggered.

On several occasions we have been minutes away from launching our bomber force. We have, fortunately, had time to identify mistakes before initiating a holocaust. The new generation of nuclear weapons would create a very different and more dangerous situation. New first-strike weapons systems (such as the MX missile) now being developed and deployed by both sides raise the possibility that in times of crisis, there will be the temptation to use them for a preemptive strike to knock out the enemy's missiles before they can be launched. The installation of these weapons would likely cause computers on both sides to be programmed to "launch on warning," thus dramatically increasing the chances of war by electronic error. With Soviet and NATO missiles aimed at each other across relatively short distances in Europe, both sides could find themselves with less than six minutes to determine if an attack is real or only another false warning.

As more and more countries develop nuclear weapons, the probability of nuclear war increases. Few of us have contemplated the implications of nuclear weapons in the hands of Israel, the Arab states, Pakistan, South Africa, and dozens of other nations, yet that day could arrive soon. Today, as many as thirty-five nations have the technological capacity to produce nuclear bombs. Before the year 2000, many of these nations could elect to join the nuclear weapons club. Consider also the nightmarish possibility of nuclear weapons in the hands of dictators of unstable Third World countries or maniacal terrorists who would stop at nothing to achieve their aims.

This "horizontal proliferation" of nuclear weapons offers

ever more extensive opportunities for nuclear conflicts and accidents. It increases the likelihood that the United States and the Soviet Union could be catalyzed by a third power into a nuclear war. We could even see the day when an American city would be annihilated without our knowing who delivered the bomb.

As long as the two superpowers continue to expand their nuclear arsenals, there is little hope that other nations can be dissuaded from joining the nuclear club. As Congressman Ed Markey has stated:

If the United States and the Soviet Union believe they can employ weapons in a limited, rational manner to coerce one another, why can't India and Pakistan believe the same? If the United States and the Soviet Union believe that nuclear war is survivable and winnable, why can't Brazil and Argentina believe the same?

Only a mutual agreement between the two superpowers to stop and gradually reverse the arms race could lead to the strict measures needed to prevent nuclear weapons from spreading throughout the world. (Both the U.S. and the U.S.S.R. formally promised to take such action in Article VI of the Nuclear Non-Proliferation Treaty of 1968.)

The growing threat of accidental nuclear war and the danger inherent in horizontal proliferation are the inevitable by-products of the policy of attempting to prevent nuclear war by preparing for nuclear war. This should cause us to question whether we can continue indefinitely to base our hopes for security on the risky policy of deterrence, which no one seems willing to define, and which strikes some as a semantic smoke screen to conceal a futile quest for superiority.

It should be apparent that the strategy of maintaining peace through terror has severe limitations. The balance of terror dictates that weapons be built and deployed not for use, but rather to serve as symbols of a nation's power and resolve to protect itself—proof that it really means to destroy its opponent. New weapons are also developed and built to become bargaining chips, tokens of trade that can be used in arms-control negotiations. When bombs and missiles become symbols or chips, there can never be enough.

The most serious flaw of the deterrence strategy, however, is that it only has to fail once. There is no second chance. The argument that deterrence has worked—that we have not yet had a nuclear war—is not unlike the boast of the three-pack-a-day cigarette smoker that he has not yet died of cancer. The fact that we have been extraordinarily lucky up to now should not encourage us to push our luck much further.

It is equally unwise to hope that someday soon a technological breakthrough will save us. There is not now, nor is there ever likely to be, any defense against nuclear weapons. When President Reagan proposed a space-based ballistic-missile defense system in 1983, Rear Admiral Eugene J. Carroll, Jr. (Ret.), a specialist on the subject, stated that such devices would increase the chances of accidental nuclear war and assure that any hostilities in space would merely be a prelude to the war on earth. Admiral Carroll concluded that "weapons in space will not enhance our national security or secure space for peaceful purposes. Space is not an arena into which man can transfer his vices and ignore the consequences on earth."

If we can learn anything from nearly four decades of the nuclear arms race, it should be apparent by now that neither the United States nor the Soviet Union will ever permit its adversary to gain the advantage. Furthermore, each nation will spend whatever it takes to keep up with the other. For more than fifty years, the Soviets have deprived the consumer sector of their society to favor of military spending, and they show no sign of retreating from that course. Similarly, the United States continues to divert a large and growing portion of its resources and talent to the military in pursuit of the illusion that the next weapon, or the next, or the next, will give us superiority and security.

But are we secure when there is nothing we can do to prevent our homes, our offices, our factories, our families, indeed our entire country, from becoming, in a matter of hours, a smoldering pile of radioactive ashes? Are we secure when our only "protection" lies in our ability to inflict even greater devastation on our opponent?

In the vain pursuit of an unachievable illusion, nuclear superiority, we have lost sight of the critical fact that preparing for war leads to war. When in history has it been otherwise? Lord Mountbatten, one of the most brilliant military leaders of World War II, said in 1979:

> There are powerful voices around the world who still repeat the old Roman precept—if you desire peace, prepare for war. This is absolute nuclear nonsense. A war can hardly fail to involve the all-out use of nuclear weapons. Such a war would be over in a matter of days. And when it is over, who and what would be left? . . . a few mutilated survivors with no hospitals, no help, no hope.

Neither participant can win—but both can lose—the race to oblivion.

SENATOR PROXMIRE: What do you think is the prospect, then, of nuclear war?

ADMIRAL H. G. RICKOVER: I think we will probably destroy ourselves. . . .

A report released May 10, 1983, by the World Health Organization estimates that about half the world's population of 4.5 billion would be "immediate victims" of an all-out nuclear war—1.5 billion dead and 1.1 billion injured survivors whose chances of receiving any medical attention would be "next to nil." The report states that "devastation to the advanced economies of the world would be virtually complete." All sectors of the interrelated economic network—money, banking, investment—would collapse, and even the simplest aspects of commerce or production would be impossible.

FIVE

The Decline of America

DESPITE THE OBVIOUS and growing danger posed by the nuclear arms race, the management of our national enterprise continues to pursue a policy of preventing nuclear war by preparing for it. Aside from the peril it places us in, our increasing dependence on nuclear weapons as a means of maintaining our security has other serious consequences for our national enterprise. It affects our economy, our influence in the world, and our morale as a nation.

Business leaders are uniquely qualified to evaluate the impact of our national security policy and assess its efficacy. In examining any policy, people who make business decisions are trained to get to the heart of the matter, to lay aside dogma, tradition, and justifications in order to ask the basic, bottom-line question: Does it work? As a consultant to the American enterprise, it is appropriate for you to examine our national security policy with the following questions in mind: Does it achieve its objectives? Has it taken into account changing realities? Do the benefits derived justify the real costs and potential consequences? What is the overall impact of the policy on our country?

True national security requires a strong economy, yet today the once-firm foundation of America's economic strength and superiority is crumbling rapidly. Our stagnating economy is characterized by unprecedented federal deficits, high unemployment, and declining industrial productivity and innovation. Our competitors are marketing better products for lower prices, challenging what once was our unquestioned supremacy in the world marketplace.

Not surprisingly, because American economic strength has been on the decline, it appears that our prestige in the world is also diminishing. Since the war in Vietnam, the United States has suffered a series of setbacks in its attempts to extend its influence in the world community. A vacillating foreign policy has confused our friends as well as our adversaries, and our vast military power has often been rendered impotent. Our multibillion-dollar nuclear arsenal remains unusable unless we are willing to commit national suicide.

Accompanying the decline in American economic and political power is a sense of malaise that seems to infect our entire body politic. The spirit of confidence and optimism once so characteristic of Americans has given way to doubt and confusion. There is the general and demoralizing awareness that this nation is not what it used to be and may never be again.

Attempts have been made to understand, explain, and justify the American decline in many ways, but these examinations have rarely taken into account the effects of the nuclear arms race and our preparations for nuclear war. Similarly, preoccupation with the military aspect of our national security has prevented us from considering other, equally fundamental aspects of security—economic strength, global influence, and national morale—the areas in which the decline of America is most apparent. How has the arms race affected these vital security needs?

Since World War II, American military spending has totaled more than 3 trillion dollars, with many billions going to the development, production, and deployment of nuclear weapons. The generally accepted view has been that this massive military spending has been a boon to the American economy. Now, however, leading economists and business experts (among them Lester Thurow of M.I.T., Charles Schultz, former chairman of the Council of Economic Advisers under President Carter, and Murray Weidenbaum, former chairman of President Reagan's Council of Economic Advisers) are challenging this assumption. Excessive military spending is not a prescription for prosperity, it is being said. Rather, it contributes directly to our economic woes. The continuing escalation of the arms race bears directly on the major aspects of the economic problems that continue to plague us: unemployment, foreign competition, low productivity, and slow technological progress.

Some economists are now making a convincing argument that over the past three decades, military spending (which has averaged about 30 percent of the entire federal budget and nearly 50 percent of discretionary funds) has contributed significantly to American economic decline. What may blind us to the relationship between our stagnating economy and our astronomical military expenditures is the enduring myth that military spending is good for business. The fact that World War II followed the Great Depression had the indelible effect of convincing many that military spending creates jobs and improves productivity. It was the war, they believe, that got us producing again.

It is very likely, however, that if the astronomical sums spent during World War II had been invested in *anything* in the economy, there would have been the same result. Still, the notion that the war ended the Depression and the fact that after the war prosperity was accompanied by high military spending convinced Americans that what's good for the Pentagon is good for the economy. (Those who still cling to this myth might be considered "Marxist Capitalists"—people who seem to agree with the theory of Karl Marx that capitalism could not survive without spending for war or its equivalent in military appropriations.)

At the root of this myth is a massive misunderstanding about the nature of military products as opposed to other economic products. In contrast to consumer and producer goods, military goods neither add directly to the present standard of living nor increase the productivity of the economic system. Dollars spent on weapons, tanks, fighter planes, and submarines are dead-end dollars. They consume enormous quantities of valuable resources but put nothing back into the economic system. Therefore, military spending may in the short term stimulate employment and purchasing power, but in the long run it drains the economy.

Although these expenditures do not produce goods and services, they do inject money into the economy that is spent on consumer and producer goods and services. This creates the classic inflationary situation in which there is too much money chasing after too few goods. While most people assume it was the OPEC oil-price increases that initiated the spiral of inflation in the 1970's, the fact is that heavy military expenditures, including the cost of the war in Vietnam, first fueled the inflationary fires, beginning in the mid-1960's. By 1969, four years before OPEC, the rate of inflation had already tripled.

Military procurement methods also contribute to inflation. Unlike the real world of market-oriented business, in the world of military contracts jobs are performed on a cost-plus basis. This means that after-cost profits are guaranteed regardless of inefficient operations, questionable overhead expenses, and other cost overruns. Although there are supposed to be cost-effectiveness incentives, they are poorly applied, and a firm that knows its profits are assured regardless of what happens has little incentive to keep costs as low as possible.

In addition to the direct inflationary consequences, high military spending produces an equally serious long-term effect: the severe deterioration of our civilian technological base. Once this country was the world leader in the development of new products and innovative production methods. American know-how and technological ingenuity were envied and emulated throughout the world. In the past two decades, however, the U.S. has fallen far behind other countries in the rate of technological progress. This erosion of economic vitality in the civilian sector is due in large measure to the fact that the military sector claims 30 to 50 percent of all the scientists and engineers in America.

With less technology and brainpower applied to civilian industrial problems and challenges, U.S. industry has lost the capacity it once had to innovate and to absorb increasing costs by increasing efficiency. It has become common practice in many fields of business to pass cost increases on to the consumer. This "cost-pass-along" policy produces a cycle of higher prices, continued inflation, and more unemployment.

The lack of civilian scientists and engineers has also contributed greatly to the decline in competitive capability of U.S. industries in the world market. In the past fifteen years, our position as the world's undisputed industrial leader has declined rapidly. Foreign competitors, particularly Japan and West Germany, have made massive inroads into the automobile, steel, and commercial electronics markets.

Is it merely coincidental that both Japan and West Germany have had low levels of military spending, or that both countries invest comparatively low percentages of their research-and-development expenditures for military purposes? While two thirds of our federal R & D funds go to the military, West Germany spends only 15 to 20 percent and the Japanese less than 5 percent. Similarly, much of our investment capital is absorbed by the military. In the U.S., out of every hundred dollars of capital available for domestic investment, $46 goes to the military. In West Germany, the figure is $14 and in Japan only $3.70.

Supporters of massive military budgets argue that military-related research transfers to the civilian sector and that everyone benefits from breakthroughs in weapons research. Evidence indicates, however, that this spillover has been marginal, and that spin-offs are generally quite costly. For the most part, the diversion of technical talent to the military has had a negative impact on American industrial innovation. While Japanese engineers were developing solid-state circuitry for an array of commercial electronic products, American engineers were perfecting the electronics of sophisticated missile systems.

The argument is often made that military spending creates jobs and that reductions in the Pentagon budget would add to unemployment. This point bears examination since it often appears that debates over new weapons systems have more to do with the jobs involved than with the actual need for the systems. A growing number of economists now maintain, however, that military spending actually generates *unemployment* by diverting resources from the civilian economy.

Research conducted by Employment Research Associates and corroborated by U.S. Labor Department statistics shows that increases in the military budget have actually reduced employment opportunities. The money the Pentagon spends goes primarily for equipment and to highly skilled workers. On the average, a billion dollars spent for military purposes generates far fewer jobs (eighteen thousand) than the same billion dollars spent in the civilian industrial sector (twenty-seven thousand). If those funds were available for investment in the private sector, they would create more jobs in areas where they are most needed. The research indicates that in every area—consumer products, investment, and state and local government—nonmilitary expenditures create more jobs than does military spending.

Excellent products, technological progress, and high productivity once distinguished the United States among the in-

dustrial nations of the world. But the long-term diversion of
capital and labor to weapons production has sapped our
civilian industrial strength. A recent study by the Council on
Economic Priorities compares thirteen major industrialized
countries and shows that those which spent a smaller share of
their economic output for military purposes generally had
much stronger economies with higher productivity, more investment, and faster growth. The United States, the Soviet
Union, and Britain, the three nations with the heaviest military burden, have economies that are seriously stagnating.

This is not to say that massive military spending is the only
cause of America's economic problems or to suggest that the
nation should neglect its legitimate security needs. But there
is ample reason to question whether the hundreds of billions
of dollars—along with the "brain drain"—diverted to create
still more nuclear weapons add up to a sensible investment in
genuine national security.

President Eisenhower's words on this subject are particularly appropriate in this context:

There is no way in which a country can satisfy the crav-
ing for absolute security—but it can bankrupt itself,
morally and economically, in attempting to reach that
illusory goal through arms alone. The military establishment, not productive of itself, necessarily must feed on
the energy, productivity, and brain power of the country, and if it takes too much, our total strength declines.

. . . Every gun that is made, every warship launched,
every rocket fired, signifies in the final sense a theft from
those who are hungry and are not fed, those who are cold
and are not clothed. This world in arms is not spending
money alone. It is spending the sweat of its laborers, the
genius of its scientists, the hopes of its children.

It is time for business leaders to lead the American people in asking whether the safety of their streets and neighborhoods, the quality of their schools, and the security of their jobs are not real aspects of national security that should be weighed against the illusion of safety produced by an absurdly excessive quantity of nuclear weapons. It is time to decide whether or not national security can exist without economic security. It is time for straight talk by business people—in which they tell their elected representatives and their fellow citizens that the pursuit of unachievable nuclear superiority is the essence of bad business and a sure prescription for national disaster.

The 3 trillion dollars spent since World War II for so-called security might be considered a worthwhile investment if the American people got what they paid for. The fact is that with thousands of nuclear weapons "protecting" us, few feel secure. Each advance in military technology reduces the number of minutes in which we can be totally destroyed by design, miscalculation, or the failure of a computer chip. Something is screwy. It's time to ask: Who's in charge here?

No one would ever contend that military power is useless. Nevertheless, I wish to emphasize that our myopic "militaritis"—our excessive dependence on military solutions to nonmilitary problems—has prevented us from recognizing and responding rationally to the far-reaching changes in the world around us. The decline of American power is not, as some have argued, the result of military weakness. The United States is still the strongest military power in the world. But many factors, including the end of colonialism and the rise of nationalism in the Third World, changing economic forces, and shifts in power distribution, have ended forever the days when the United States could function as the preeminent policeman of the world community.

The prenuclear notion that more weapons means more

power is in part responsible for the belief that spending more money on the military or using our military more aggressively can reverse the decline of American power. But the forces at work in the world today call for new approaches. Now, however, our preoccupation with military strategies is preventing us from developing political and economic strategies that could work to help solve global problems and reestablish American preeminence, prestige, and constructive influence.

Even if we never use any of the weapons in our massively redundant nuclear arsenal, we will inflict tremendous damage on ourselves. As our economy stumbles and as our cities, neighborhoods, and schools deteriorate, the quality of American life declines. Increasingly, unemployment destroys the spirit of people who want nothing more than to work for a living. Recognizing that this kind of emotional and psychological damage can be just as devastating as war, it seems appropriate to examine the effect the nuclear arms race has on that critical, if intangible, element we call our national spirit.

Living in the shadow of nuclear war, where at any time the fireball can descend upon us and destroy all that we have created, we seem to have lost the energetic and determined optimism once so characteristic of the American people. Without a bomb being dropped, we are already suffering a sort of psychic radiation sickness—a frame of mind that affects every aspect of our lives.

A poll taken in California in 1982 showed that 85 percent of the respondents believed there would be a nuclear war in their lifetime and about the same percentage believed they would not survive. The conviction that nuclear war is inevitable is particularly acute among children and young people. Their fears of the future, indeed of having *no future*, permeate their lives and attitudes, depriving them of the fundamental right of childhood: looking forward to growing up, planning for participation in life, and dreaming of future enjoyment and accomplishment. It is not surprising, then, that so many young people are troubled, directionless, and hopeless, or that there is an alarming rise in drug abuse and suicides.

Even if a nuclear holocaust does not occur, psychic radiation sickness is already taking a heavy toll in all sectors of our society, but especially in the business world, for young people who perceive themselves to be the final generation are unlikely to be motivated to prepare for their future. For me, as a businessman, it is terrifying to reflect on the following words:

> The American Psychiatric Association recently studied one thousand adolescents in Boston and Los Angeles and found, to their horror, that almost all of those children believe that they will never have jobs, that they will never get married or have children, because they are almost certainly going to be killed in a nuclear war.

The nuclear weapons race is robbing our nation of its most precious resource, its spirit. Without a sense that there is a future in which we can see ourselves learning, growing, achieving, procreating, we find ourselves slowly losing our will to survive. For if we accept that nuclear war is inevitable, we must be willing, eventually, to give up our efforts to prevent it. Or even if we believe that more and more weapons will stave off war indefinitely, we must live with the responsibility of managing a force that can destroy all of life. That kind of responsibility requires a vigilance and commitment that cannot reasonably be expected of continuing generations.

Rather than protecting us, a national security policy based on nuclear weapons represents the greatest threat to our security. A businesslike assessment of our present policy indicates that it is in the best interest of our national enterprise to find alternatives to the nuclear arms race.

Clearly, most Americans would favor new policies that would reverse the decline of our national power. They would prefer to reduce our nuclear arsenal, cut military spending, and commit more resources to the civilian economy were it not for the fear that such decisions would leave the United States and its allies vulnerable to the aggressive aims of our perceived enemy, the Soviet Union. Americans want a way out, but there is always the question: What about the Russians?

In a moment of private candor at Camp David in 1959, President Eisenhower confessed to Nikita Khrushchev that every time he tried to cut defense funds he would end up by backing down before aggressive military advisers who warned him that the Russians were developing new weapons systems which would reduce the United States to a second-rate power.

Khrushchev, according to his memoirs, replied, "It's just the same. Some people from our military department come and say, Comrade Khrushchev, look at this. The Americans are developing such and such a system. And we take the steps which our military people have recommended."

—SENATOR J. WILLIAM FULBRIGHT
November 1974

SIX

A New Look at the Competition

WHEN WE LOOK AT the world situation in terms of our business model, we see USA, Inc. sacrificing a major portion of its money, manpower, and material in order to protect itself against the incursion of its chief competitor. This policy is not only severely limiting the company's ability to conduct business, it is economically damaging, morally debilitating, and dangerously counterproductive. It actually increases the threat it is intended to protect against.

Why has the most powerful nation in human history chosen such a destructive, self-defeating, and dangerous course? To those who adhere to this policy, the answer is simple: We have no choice. They believe that the threat posed by the Soviet Union makes it absolutely impossible to stop, reduce, or alter our expanding dependence on nuclear weapons and military power.

These beliefs, pressed upon the American mind for decades, have driven us to pursue the illusory security of nuclear superiority. We have been taught to believe that unless we have a constantly expanding nuclear arsenal to stop them, atheistic Communist hordes will surely sweep across the face of the earth. They would take over every nation on earth, wiping out every vestige of freedom, enslaving millions to live under the oppressive yoke of totalitarianism. The result would be a grim, empty, lifeless world devoid of freedom, passion, or hope. There has been conjured up in our minds the terrifying image of the Godless, heartless Communist leader with his finger poised over the nuclear button, waiting and watching for the smallest sign of weakness on our part. These are the paranoid images of our Russophobia.

Over the past two generations, politicians have been able to funnel trillions of tax dollars and five hundred billion man-hours into the military, by stoking the fires of our mortal fear of the monolithic Soviet Communist conspiracy. Beginning in the late 1940's, when Senator Vandenberg advised President Truman that the only way to get money for the military was "to scare the hell out of the American public," we have been subjected to reports about "bomber gaps," then "missile gaps," and most recently, a "window of vulnerability." In each case, frightened American taxpayers have allowed billions of their tax dollars to close the gaps and shut the windows, only to find that there were no such emergencies in the first place.

With the Soviet threat as the primary animating force behind America's participation in the nuclear weapons race, with the costs skyrocketing, and with the fate of the entire world hanging in the balance, it seems sensible at this point to ask the question: What exactly is the nature of the Soviet threat?

With the stakes of this competition extraordinarily high, it would seem imperative that we know as much as possible about our competitor. Yet with regard to the Soviet Union, its history, its government, its people, and its problems, we are woefully ignorant, uninformed, and, some say, tragically misled.

Obviously, Soviet society is diametrically different from that of the United States: Theirs is a centrally planned, state-controlled economic system; an autocratic, one-party political hierarchy run by a small Communist-party elite. It is an officially atheistic society in which every aspect of people's individual lives is monitored, directed, and controlled in some way by the state.

Such a society, without the personal rights and freedoms taken for granted in Western democracies, is naturally repugnant to Americans. We wonder how the Russians are able to tolerate such a repressive system. What we overlook is that the Russian people, never having known the democratic traditions of the West, simply have no experience with the ideas and values we consider basic.

This profound difference has led some American politicians to characterize the Russian people as evil, a diabolically aggressive and malevolent force in the world. This devil image is the kind of dangerous oversimplification that has confused and misled Americans for decades and continues to fuel a potentially fatal nuclear arms race neither side can ever win.

Certainly Soviet communism is morally repugnant to us and its international conduct politically loathsome. Nevertheless, we have coexisted with the present Soviet system for over sixty years. Now that co-extinction threatens us both, does it make sense, in terms of our own self-interest, to paint our differences black and white and wage a rhetorical holy war against the Russians?

Before we can deal rationally with the Russian challenge, we must also remind ourselves that the world situation is never static and that our perceptions of "the enemy" can change quite rapidly. It wasn't long after World War II that the Germans and Japanese, whom we hated and feared with the same intense passion we now reserve for the Russians, became our closest allies and friends. In the early 1970's, we witnessed the transformation of China from mortal foe to almost-friend.

Much earlier, it was apparent that the Communist threat was not so monolithic, that China pursued her own particular brand of communism very different from the Soviet version, as have other Communist countries such as Hungary, Albania, Yugoslavia, and Vietnam. Indeed, with the Chinese snubbing the Russians and making friendly overtures to the West, it could be said that we have more Communists on our side than the Russians have on their side.

Obviously, our world situation can change so rapidly that it seems absurd to prepare for nuclear war on the basis that our current "enemy" gives us no alternative. But when we are told that our enemy is the "focus of evil in the modern world" or that we would be "better dead than Red," we tend to forget what our options are.

If we want to survive, we must recognize that thermonuclear technology has transformed the U.S. and the U.S.S.R. into global Siamese twins. If one of us attempts to destroy the other, we will both perish together.

It is vital to our survival that we reassess our relationship with the Soviet Union using a fundamental principle of sound business practice: Know the competition. Up to now, we have based our Soviet policies solely on their military inventory and the rhetoric of their leaders. But, as in any business enterprise, we need to know not merely what they say they want, but what they can actually accomplish. We need to take into account their weaknesses and their failures, the legacy of their historical experience, as well as the impact the changing world is having on their economy, their culture, and their expectations for the future. Let's begin with a brief historical perspective.

Living Americans have never experienced the devastation of a war in our homeland, so we have little appreciation of the wartime experience of the Russian people. This perspective is fundamental, however, to gaining insight into the nature of

Soviet intentions and capabilities. Suspicion, distrust, and paranoia are characteristic of the Russian mentality, and if we trace recent Russian history, it is not difficult to understand why.

Three times in this century the Russian homeland has been invaded: first by the Germans in World War I; then in 1920 by a force from fourteen nations (including our own) seeking to crush the Bolshevik Revolution; and again by the Nazis who destroyed seventy-three thousand Russian cities, towns, and villages and caused the death of more than twenty million people, one tenth of the Russian population. Virtually no Russian family escaped this murderous experience, and its emotional and psychological wounds have been slow to heal.

The scars left by the devastation of World War II may make it easier to understand why the Soviets refused to give up control of the territory they occupied after the war. To us, Soviet occupation of Eastern Europe and the subsequent establishment of satellite regimes was an aggressive and expansionistic action. To the Russians, it was a defensive and self-protective strategy, designed to create a buffer zone against the possibility of yet another invasion from the West.

We need not condone the Soviets' abhorrent occupation of Eastern Europe, but merely put it into historical perspective. We must recognize that the horrors of the past feed the fears of the Russian population and also make it easier for Soviet leaders to manipulate the people's paranoia and justify the crushing burden of their military policy.

Throughout four decades of Cold War there have been essentially two divergent views of the Soviet Union in the United States. One view leads to the continuing escalation of the arms race, while the other opens up a new and quite different way of thinking about the Russians. The traditional view is that the Soviet Union is an inherently aggressive nation fully capable of carrying out its evil intentions. Another view is that the Soviets are essentially defense-oriented and lack the political, economic, or military power to carry out the threats of their aggressive rhetoric.

These two views have been delineated by a man acknowledged and respected as a foremost expert in Soviet affairs, former Ambassador to the Soviet Union George F. Kennan. The two perspectives, says Ambassador Kennan, are not dissimilar with regard to the facts. They differ, however, as to how the facts are interpreted and as to what action should be taken as a result of those interpretations.

The view of the Soviets as aggressive generally holds that Russia is a brutal, totalitarian state bent on, and capable of, world domination through military power. Those who see the Soviet Union as a potent and utterly evil threat, the mortal enemy of freedom, come to the following conclusions regarding Soviet strategy and intentions:

- Soviet leaders seek expansion of their power at the expense of other nations and world stability and peace. They relish upheaval and will stop short of nothing, even nuclear war, to achieve power.

- The Russians have conducted and continue to conduct a massive military buildup for aggressive rather than defensive purposes.

- Soviet strategy is to foment revolution where none would otherwise occur and to dominate Third World countries and use them as pawns in struggles with the West.

- The internal difficulties of the Soviet state are not serious enough to deter their expansionist actions.

- The Russians cannot be trusted to negotiate in good faith or to keep any international agreements.

It follows, then, that proponents of this view see only conflict and confrontation with the Soviet Union. They believe that the only way to meet the Soviet challenge is with military power. They refuse to acknowledge that there is relative parity in U.S. and Soviet military strength, but instead claim that U.S. military forces are inferior. They call on Americans to rearm to "catch up with the Russians," and thus be able to deter the inevitable Soviet aggression.

Another view of the Soviets is the one subscribed to by Ambassador Kennan himself and shared by former Ambassador to the Soviet Union Averell Harriman. Their perspective is based on a perception of the Soviet leadership not as warmongers, but rather as men motivated primarily by defensive considerations. This is what they see:

- While the Soviets may wish to expand their *influence* in the world, there is no evidence that they would want to invade Western Europe or the United States or add to the countries under their authority.

- The Soviets see themselves as encircled by hostile powers. (Indeed, every nuclear weapon outside the Soviet Union, except those on Russian submarines, is *aimed at* the Soviet Union.) At least 25 percent of their military forces are positioned along their forty-five-hundred-mile border with China.

- Internal problems throughout Russia—failure in agriculture, worker apathy and absenteeism, corruption, alcoholism, and increasing minority unrest—claim primary attention of the Russian leadership. These problems are exacerbated by huge military expenditures.

- The Russians have, in almost every instance, adhered to specific treaty agreements with the U.S.

What emerges from this view is a picture of the Russians as highly insecure, isolated, and defensive, saddled with a crushing military burden resulting from their determination to "keep up with the Americans." Proponents of this perspective argue that the U.S. must take into account the weaknesses of the Soviet system and not merely focus on Russian military strength. They assume that the Russian leadership would welcome reductions in weapons competition that would enable them to redirect their resources to the civilian sector, which is hungry for better food and more consumer goods.

The view of the Soviet Union as primarily self-protective might make more sense to us if we looked at the actions of the United States from their point of view. A Russian looking at America's Cold War conduct sees the United States as a nation that:

1) has consistently been the first to initiate new weapons that accelerate the nuclear arms race;
2) has refused to ratify the terms of the second Strategic Arms Limitation Treaty (SALT II) already agreed to by the Soviet Union;
3) has refused to agree to a policy of "no first use" of nuclear weapons and is now actively engaged in developing first-strike weapons and war plans;
4) maintains five hundred thousand troops stationed in more than three hundred bases and military installations around the world and uses military aid and advisers in more than sixty countries;
5) sends its troops to fight halfway around the world in places such as Vietnam, yet condemns the Soviet Union for sending troops into bordering Afghanistan;
6) has stated that it considers limited nuclear war feasible and winnable, and has publicly threatened countries

with nuclear war at least a dozen times in the past thirty years.

Given this Soviet view of the United States, is it not possible that they consider the American threat to be as dangerous as we consider the Russian threat? Is it not possible that we both attribute to the other the threatening intentions and actions that make us each defensive? Isn't it time to question the fundamental issue of this extremely dangerous game?

What, specifically, is the Soviet threat? Experts seem to agree at least on the areas of conflict, if not the degree of danger posed. It seems apparent that in terms of geopolitical strategies, the Soviet Union seeks to:

1) pursue equal superpower status with the U.S., both politically and militarily;
2) maintain political and military control of its "buffer zone" in Eastern Europe and expand its political and economic influence in Western Europe;
3) displace Western influence in the Third World by supporting struggles for national liberation;
4) assert its dominance in the Communist world by restraining the influence of China.

The least likely occurrence is a direct attack on the United States in an attempt to conquer us by force of arms. In fact, the Soviet Union seeks to avoid a military confrontation with the United States since it would be a direct threat to the above objectives. It is generally agreed that the major Soviet challenges to the U.S. are in Europe and the Third World.

Since 1945, Europe has remained the primary focus of U.S.–Soviet relations. Now, with smoldering unrest in Poland and increasing opposition to the deployment of additional nuclear weapons in NATO countries, there is concern that instabilities are threatening the political alliances of NATO and the Warsaw Pact and could lead to a dangerous military confrontation.

We know that the Soviets are serious about maintaining their buffer zone and will use military invasion to keep control as they have done in Hungary, in Czechoslovakia, and, most recently, in Afghanistan. But given the burden of the protective armor they have built up around themselves, it is unlikely they would want to expand it. If the Russians are having a difficult time maintaining their authority in Poland, imagine what they would have to contend with in Italy or France! Furthermore, what would such an attack accomplish for the Soviets, given the fact of formidable NATO forces and the probability of a recourse to nuclear weapons by the Western powers? Does not a Russian invasion of Western Europe, when looked at rationally, seem fairly implausible?

Admiral Gene LaRocque (Ret.) of the Center for Defense Information has stated:

> I do not believe that at any time there has been any evidence to suggest that the Soviets were planning to launch a military attack on the U.S. or Western Europe. There has been no time in their history when the Soviets would have had anything to gain from an attack on the U.S. or Europe, nor can I visualize any set of circumstances when it would be to their advantage. Soviet officials have never evidenced any illusions about the mortal danger they would put themselves in by such action. They have never shown any confidence that Soviet military power is such as to even raise the prospect of success in such a war.

As for expanding their influence in the Third World, the Soviets have, with the exception of Cuba, been notoriously unsuccessful. We tend to forget that Soviet communism is very different from the many other brands of communism that find supporters in the developing nations. Nowhere in the world is the Soviet model admired and emulated. Even though Soviet-supported military interventions in the Third World have increased, they have not resulted in increased Soviet influence. Where rapport once existed, as in China, Egypt, Indonesia, Somalia, and Ghana—the Russians have either been summarily ejected, or certainly overstayed their welcome.

A grave misunderstanding of Third World nationalist revolutions by the United States has led us to believe that what is at stake in these countries is "stopping communism." Although the Soviet Union has been quite willing to offer military and economic aid in support of revolutionary forces, it does not mean that these forces are Communist-inspired or Communist-led. In many cases, nationalist revolutionary elements have turned to the Soviets for aid only because it was refused by the U.S. This was true for Ho Chi Minh in Vietnam, for Castro in Cuba, and for the new Sandinista regime in Nicaragua. In many instances, Soviet influence in the Third World might be considered more a function of American failures than Soviet successes.

A realistic picture of Soviet adventurism in the Third World shows that the Russians as neocolonialists have fared worse than we have. Out of 155 countries about 19 owe allegiance to the Soviet Union. A reliable study of "Soviet Geopolitical Momentum" (January 1980) shows that Soviet influence throughout the world has not only decreased since the 1950's, it is dwarfed by the U.S. and its allies, which command 70 percent of the world's military and economic power.

Since 1980, the Soviet Union has kept a relatively low profile in the Third World, probably because of the drain of its military stalemate in Afghanistan, pressing economic problems, and concern about its relationships with Poland, China, and the United States.

What has become of the stated Soviet policy of exporting Communist revolution throughout the world? Ambassador Kennan makes the case that while "world revolution remains basic to Marxist ideology and Russian rhetoric, it has ceased to figure as a serious immediate goal of policy." Whatever Russia's aims might be with regard to world domination, the real issue is whether they are *capable* of doing what they say they want to do.

While it has achieved relative parity in nuclear weapons, the Soviet Union lacks the capability to expand militarily in the Third World. According to a 1979 report by the U.S. Joint Chiefs of Staff, the Soviets do not have marine forces, a naval-carrier force, air-transport force, or air- or ground-support systems necessary to such operations. A 1979 Rand Corporation study also concluded that the Soviets could not support an invasion beyond their immediate border states and that "Soviet capabilities to project power abroad do not remotely equal the United States."

It is increasingly apparent that nationalist forces within the Third World reject both Soviet and American domination. Iran should be but one good example of the fact that revolutionary nationalism spurns the influence of both superpowers. Certainly, Soviet communism has proved to have little appeal to the developing world. In sum, it seems less likely now that the Third World will become the scene of major U.S.–Soviet military conflict, but it will no doubt remain an area for competition.

The most dangerous aspect of Soviet–American competition is not Russian expansionism, but an out-of-control nuclear weapons race with a life of its own apart from the threat of either adversary, real or imagined.

The two adversaries seem to be deadlocked over the issue of military parity, some Americans charging that a massive Russian buildup has created Soviet superiority, and the Soviet Union asserting that while they are content with a relative parity of forces, the U.S. keeps upping the ante in order to maintain its superiority. Accompanying these claims are charges by each side that the other is developing a first-strike capability and preparing to fight and win an all-out nuclear war. These positions continue to prevent progress in U.S.– Soviet relations and in efforts to negotiate reductions in the overkill capacity of both arsenals.

But there is a way out of the nuclear impasse. It lies in our willingness to recognize that the United States and the Soviet Union now face a common enemy, nuclear annihilation. In the aftermath of nuclear war, who will be able to distinguish the ashes of communism from those of capitalism? Certainly, our two competing systems are different, but is there anything at stake between us that could possibly be worth the assured mutual destruction of a nuclear war?

Two decades ago, President John F. Kennedy spoke of our relationship with the Soviet Union and called upon the American people "not to see conflict as inevitable, accommodation as impossible, and communication as nothing more than an exchange of threats." In asking Americans for a new spirit of good faith and in calling for a creative and conciliatory diplomacy, Kennedy reminded us that "if we cannot end now our differences, at least we can help make the world safe for diversity." Businesslike application of enlightened self-interest makes such a reasoned approach even more appropriate now.

A realistic assessment of the challenge offered by our competitor, the Soviet Union, must reveal that our conflicts of interest and even of ideology are not nearly as great as the common troubles and challenges we both face. Both societies confront critical economic and environmental problems.

Pressing upon both nations are the frustrated ambitions of the people of the Third World—three fourths of the population of the planet—whose hunger, poverty, and desperation threaten the economy and security of the entire world.

There is a way in which the United States and the Soviet Union can address common problems, control conflicts, coexist, and still compete as rival economic and political systems. If we can manage, as we have done successfully in the past, to remove the poisonous fear and hatred we attach to the enemy and consider the Soviet Union as an adversary with limited capabilities, we can engage that adversary in a new kind of competition—one that we can win.

If we allow communism to carry the banner of reform, then the ignored and the dispossessed, the insulted and injured, will turn to it as the only way out of their misery.

If we allow ourselves to become allied with those to whom the cry of "communism" is only an excuse for the perpetuation of privilege, if we assist, with military material and other aid to prevent reform for their people—then we will give the Communists a strength which they cannot attain themselves.

—ROBERT F. KENNEDY
1965

If we get sufficiently interlaced economically, we will most probably not bomb each other off the face of the planet. For example, I suggest that we are so economically intertwined with Japan that if we have any problems with Japan today, we are going to work them out. I think the same will be true globally. We should welcome increased trade with the Soviet Union, all the developed nations, and the Third World, as world trade moves us closer to world peace.

—JOHN NAISBITT
Megatrends

SEVEN

Weapons of Peace

WHILE THE WILLINGNESS to reassess our relationship with Russia is fundamental to finding a way out of the nuclear impasse, basic political and economic issues remain at stake in the competition between the United States and the Soviet Union. Deep differences divide the two nations, and it is unlikely that either country will change radically in the near future. Superpower competition is a fact of life we are unlikely to alter in the twentieth century. What we can change, however, is the essential nature of that competition.

We have already proved our ability to compete successfully with the Soviet Union in military technology. Only by starving their consumer sector of goods and services, only by neglecting their agricultural and technological development, have they been able to keep up with us in the nuclear arms race. Meanwhile, the effects of massive military spending are beginning to show on our own economy as well, and the signs of failing health make it clear that it is time to change.

Why not "beat the Russians" at a new game, one that will invigorate our economy rather than drain it and at the same time increase the security and economic well-being of the entire world? Why not meet our adversary in the marketplace, where we cannot be matched by our major competitor? Free-enterprise democracy is clearly more creative, inventive, competent, and efficient than the Soviet system.

By shifting from military to economic competition with the Soviets, we will release capital, talent, and other vital resources that can spark a worldwide economic renaissance. By demonstrating the benefits of our democratic free-enterprise system, we can reduce the appeal of totalitarian communism in the developing countries. In the process, we will enable hundreds of millions of people to raise their standard of living, thus creating thriving new markets for our goods and services.

The first step in this ambitious program must take place here in the United States. We must get our own economic house in order. What we need is nothing less than a modern, domestic version of the Marshall Plan, the program of American economic assistance that rebuilt and revitalized Europe after World War II.

The need to rebuild our own disintegrating national infrastructure—to repair roads, bridges, railroads, as well as water and sewer systems—is reaching emergency proportions in many communities throughout the country. The public services that we depend on for the fundamentals of societal life—police, fire fighting, health care, and schools—are suffering financial problems so grave that many communities must now consider if they can afford even the most basic of these services. It is not an exaggeration to say that major American cities are in an advanced state of physical and social disintegration that poses a direct threat to the lives of their citizens.

Given the debilitating effects of excessive military spending, ending the costly and counterproductive nuclear arms race can become a historic first step in reversing America's economic decline and revitalizing our role as a world economic leader.

But America's economic recovery and growth can no

longer occur in self-contained isolation. Since World War II, this nation has become increasingly interconnected with the emerging global economy. As more foreign producers compete in the American marketplace, American business, if it is to succeed, must develop long-range trade and investment opportunities overseas. And since the traditional markets of the industrialized nations are quickly becoming saturated, our underutilized industrial capacity would benefit immensely from opportunites offered by new markets.

A great opportunity for such markets lies in the developing nations of the Third World. Africa, Asia, Latin America, the Caribbean, and the Middle East already account for 40 percent of all our exports and continue to be our fastest-growing market. The economic potential in such areas is virtually limitless.

Now, however, these potential customers are mired in poverty. Hungry and diseased, they live in conditions we could hardly imagine tolerable to human beings. Nevertheless, these people work hard, they support each other, and they dream of a better life for their children. In the past, the only real reason for helping impoverished people was that it was morally right to try to ease their misery and help them gain some hope for the future. There continues to be this moral imperative, but now it is also in our own economic self-interest to support the rapid development of the world's poor nations.

Our contribution to aid programs such as the International Monetary Fund, for example, helps poor countries pay for imports they could otherwise not afford; at the same time, their purchase of our products means increased benefits for our own economy. This kind of mutually beneficial relationship can be seen in the recent history of trade with Mexico, our third-largest trading partner. When the Mexican economy was booming in 1981, the Mexicans imported about eighteen billion dollars in American farm products and manufactured goods. But by the end of 1982, when the Mexican economy was in serious trouble, our exports fell to twelve billion dollars. This drop of six billion dollars translates into the loss of approximately a quarter-million jobs in the United States.

Expanding our trade, investment, and economic assistance in the Third World is neither charity nor altruism. It is sound business practice. Again, the Marshall Plan is an illuminating model. According to the late British economist Barbara Ward:

> The whole boom of the 1950s and the 1960s would have been inconceivable without the launching pad of the Marshall Plan, which in giving away for over five years a goodly *two* percent of a much poorer America's GNP, insured its own prosperity along with that of its neighbors in the North.

The Marshall Plan also had the effect of reducing the economic attraction of socialism and communism to the Europeans of the late 1940's. Would not an assistance program of similar dimension have the same effect now in the developing world?

There is still alive a persistent myth that the United States already gives away massive amounts of foreign economic assistance, but in truth, we rank seventeenth among developed nations in terms of the percentage of GNP that goes for economic aid. Our level of assistance to poor nations has steadily declined from one-half of one percent of GNP in 1965 to one-fifth of one percent in 1980, and half of that is actually military assistance. As our economic problems have increased, Americans have been increasingly unwilling to pay for foreign aid, believing, often rightfully so, that it was squandered by corrupt regimes or spent for unworthy projects.

Indeed, for many years our foreign aid did little to help

the poorest of the poor. Food for Peace, our giveaway program of American farm surpluses, did on occasion provide
genuine relief in famine situations, but primarily it had the
effect of lowering food prices and hurting local farmers. Similarly, the "trickle-down" approach to development—funding
industrial projects and large-scale agriculture—had little impact on mass poverty.

The decade of the 1970's, however, brought a breakthrough in the patterns of development assistance: a bottom-
up approach that is cost-effective, economically sound, and
directly addresses the needs of the very poorest people.
United Nations development organizations, in particular the
International Fund for Agricultural Development, are now
implementing highly successful credit programs that enable
small farmers to increase their productivity and provide land-
less people with the financing and skills they need to become
self-sufficient.

There now exist effective programs that can channel our
economic assistance to developing countries. Generally,
these programs are best administered by international organizations such as the United Nations or by private agencies, but
our own Agency for International Development can also have
significant impact if there are not too many strings attached.

It is unfortunate that our foreign aid, both economic and
military, has often been used to prop up dictatorships and
support governments that stand in the way of the rightful as-
pirations of their people for food and the basic needs of life.
Time and again we have misread world events because of a
faulty perception of a monolithic, aggressive Communist
movement. We have mistaken legitimate nationalistic aspira-
tions akin to our own American Revolution as having been
fomented by outside, Communist forces. We have also been
blind to the fact that these nationalist revolutions produce
very different kinds of socialism or communism and that the
revolutionary forces do not want to be dominated by either

the Soviet Union or China, but prefer to make their own way.

Interpreting every uprising as Communist-inspired and thus a threat to U.S. interests, we have chosen the certainties of dictatorship over the vagaries of revolution, believing that the *status quo*, as long as it is noncommunist, is preferable to any change.

It is almost as if we do not believe in our own system, so afraid are we of testing it out in the marketplace of ideas. We seem to have forgotten our own revolutionary heritage and the fundamental doctrine of our Declaration of Independence: When a government no longer serves the interests of its people, it is their right, indeed their duty, to overthrow that government.

Our military support of the *status quo* has at times had the effect of pushing a revolution into the Communist camp. Certainly it had that effect in Castro's Cuba and in Vietnam, where a former president of that country, General Duong Van Minh, once told me that the death and destruction rained on the Vietnamese people from American planes had created more Communists than the bombs killed. (It is revealing also that several years after our defeat in Vietnam, the nation's Communist government approached the United States for economic aid. When we refused, they turned, of course, to the Soviet Union.)

Events of the past two decades should make it clear that we cannot stand in the way of the inevitable forces of social revolution. It is unrealistic to insist that in order to receive our support, Third World countries who have no experience with the democratic tradition should immediately pattern themselves after us. We have nothing to lose—and much to gain—by being open to pluralistic revolution, even if it has socialist leanings. We should be more willing to help new regimes seeking to meet the basic legitimate needs of their people.

Lending economic rather than military support to developing nations would require that we establish a new kind of relationship with the Third World—one of partnership rather than powership. Our trade and investment policies must respect the economic priorities of our partners, and we ought not to intervene militarily or interfere in strictly internal affairs. We can and should, however, base our foreign economic assistance on a government's willingness to carry out policies aimed at ending hunger and poverty, improving political participation, and expanding social justice and human rights.

Such cooperative partnerships with developing countries could provide the United States with a legitimately earned opportunity to reduce the appeal of communism in the Third World. It would win us friends as well as customers.

Nearly one billion people—almost one fourth of the population of the planet—are victims of hunger and chronic malnutrition. The dimension of the problem of hunger is truly staggering: fifteen to twenty million hunger-related deaths every year, most of them children. This tragedy is an unnecessary one. Every nation in the world has the capacity to feed its own people, to grow sufficient food on its own land. What is needed is agricultural technology such as irrigation systems, fertilizers, pesticides, tools, tractors, and, of course, basic farming know-how.

American agricultural technology is the most advanced and effective in the world, enabling U.S. farmers to produce huge surpluses year after year. American consumers spend a smaller portion of their income on food than those of any other country in the world. Food is something we Americans take for granted; in fact, we throw away about thirteen billion tons of it every year.

To the one out of four human beings who goes to bed hungry every night, food is life's most precious gift. It is difficult for many of us to imagine a life of constant hunger and chronic malnutrition—the unrelenting, nagging ache of an empty stomach, the fear of not knowing how long the rice will last or where the next meal will come from, the shame and despair of being unable to quiet a crying baby with milk or feed a starving son or daughter.

Without food, ideologies are empty promises. When people have the means of subsistence, they are unlikely to choose repression, but until they have food, they will trade anything for something to eat.

Who can best meet the needs of the world's hungry hundreds of millions? Certainly not the Soviet Union, a country where agricultural productivity continues to stagnate and where large quantities of food must be imported to feed the Russian people. In the production of this most basic economic commodity, the United States can outperform the Soviet Union and at the same time reduce or eliminate volatile situations that too often lead to military confrontation. An example of how economic competition could supplant military competition can be seen in the recent history of the U.S. and Soviet presence in Africa.

Virtually the entire continent of Africa is caught in the grip of a deepening crisis of hunger and poverty. Twenty-two of the world's thirty-six poorest countries are African, their per capita income averaging only $329 per year. Agricultural productivity has been steadily declining while population growth rates have increased. Africa's infant mortality rates remain the highest in the world, averaging 121 per thousand. (Compare this to twelve per thousand for North America.) In several African countries, nearly one out of every five infants born dies in the first year of life. Many more die before the age of six. During the 1970's the economies of eight African nations actually shrank, and the debts of African nations grew tenfold. In short, in every measure of the quality of life, Africa is at the bottom of the scale and headed downward.

Africa has also been the scene of intense competition be-

tween the United States and the Soviet Union, primarily in
military terms. For a time, after they had cut their colonial
ties, a number of newly created African nations turned to the
United States for aid, but, generally for reasons of suspected
Communist sympathies, we turned them down. Not surprisingly, some of them then turned to the Soviet Union for
help. In fact, according to a report on Africa by David Lamb,
"Virtually every African leader who has ended up pursuing a
radical, pro-Soviet course has done so only after first seeking
help from the United States. And with few exceptions their
relations with Moscow have not been of long duration. In
Somalia, Guinea, Sudan, and Egypt, the Soviet alliance has
faded like a summer rose."

What the Soviets brought to Africa was generally military
aid—overpriced, unreliable arms—or industrial projects that
did little to reverse the declining trends in agricultural production. Citing failures of Soviet assistance in Africa, a recent
article in *The Wall Street Journal* stated that "what Africa
needed most—capital, technology, aid, and access to markets—the Soviets didn't supply." Socialism, the article continues, served Africa no better. "Central planning—on a
continent with few trained managers—meant production
slumped, mines lost money, fields stood idle. The idea of a
'social wage' rather than a wage linked to production sent
costs soaring."

Many observers now believe that Africa is turning away
from socialism and the Soviet bloc and would like increased
support from the West, particularly the United States. It is
evident that since Africa buys 10 percent of U.S. exports and
owes billions of dollars to the world's lenders—governments
and financial institutions—the United States has a strong economic self-interest in Africa's recovery and development.
Nevertheless, the United States is not offering the aid and
trade that could bring a revival to African economies. "Some-

91

body has got to start the ball rolling, and the U.S. has to do it," says Philip Ndegwa, the governor of Kenya's central bank. "The capacity is there. What isn't there is the leadership—an international point of view." Meanwhile, American military aid to African nations is increased in order to counter the Russian presence on the continent. It is difficult to imagine a more vivid example of bad business policy.

Why not use the opportunity in Africa to prove the effectiveness of a shift from military to nonmilitary competition between the Soviet Union and ourselves?

The kind of aid that could reverse Africa's economic and agricultural decline and address the basic needs of other Third World nations is relatively inexpensive—especially when compared with what the nations of the world spend for military purposes. The total of world military expenditures is approaching six hundred billion dollars per year, most of which is spent by the Soviet Union and the United States. Annual world expenditures for development aid are about twenty billion dollars. A very small fraction of what is spent on armies and armaments could transform the quality of life throughout the Third World. Experts have estimated that a fifteen-year program to end hunger and starvation throughout the world would cost about twenty billion dollars a year, totaling three hundred billion dollars. That is only one half of one year's spending for military purposes.

The U.S. Department of Defense budget for the years 1983 to 1988 calls for spending *a billion dollars a day* on the military. Imagine what a mere fraction of this money could accomplish if invested in the economic development of the Third World!

Today, the United States is the major supplier of weapons to twenty nations engaged in military conflict. The Soviet Union plays the same role in thirteen nations. Both superpowers are spending billions of dollars on a competition that can only result in greater poverty and violence in the Third World and decreased security for the entire international community.

The desire to have enough to eat has been and continues to be the primary motivation of those who have joined the sweeping social revolutions of the twentieth century. Peasants in the Philippines, Somalia, or El Salvador who do not know Karl Marx from Groucho Marx do know that their children are hungry and that new leadership might offer what they need and want most—food and land on which to grow food.

Before his retirement in June 1983 as the U.S. Army Chief of Staff, General Edward C. Meyer, speaking of the guerrilla warfare in El Salvador, stated that he believed economic assistance to be more important in solving that nation's problems than military aid. Economic assistance, he said, "is very critical because guerrilla war is based on the legitimate concerns of the people." Responding to those needs, he said, would prevent the spread of insurgency.

American food-production technology, as well as increased trade and investment, can transform the quality of life for hundreds of millions of people now living in poverty in developing countries. The Presidential Commission on World Hunger established by President Carter called on the United States to make ending hunger the primary focus of its relations with the developing world beginning in the 1980's. Their report stated:

> There are compelling moral, economic, and national security reasons for the United States Government to make the elimination of hunger the central focus of its relations with the developing world.
>
> Cast as the dominant actor within the world's food system, the United States has a unique opportunity and

responsibility to exercise its power for the common good. Such a purposeful use of U.S. power would also focus and shape the idealism and generosity that is so indigenous to the American spirit.

Food technology is not the only product in demand in the Third World. Once people know that they can feed themselves and their families, they desire our second most valuable product: freedom.

However imperfect our society may be, the American way of life is still admired and sought after. Our democratic system based on freedom and the protection of human rights excites hope in people throughout the world. The principles of our Constitution offer a genuine alternative to the grim alternatives of dictatorship and totalitarianism.

To achieve our aims and to outperform our Communist competition, we do not have to rely merely on our military might. We need only to market our best products: food and freedom, the most needed and wanted commodities in the world today. By doing so we will invigorate a stagnating world economy, increase global economic interdependence, and at the same time decrease the chances of nuclear war.

Common sense calls upon us to stop senseless spending. Does it make sense to spend still more hundreds of billions of dollars for still more devices of thermonuclear destruction? Common sense tells us to rely instead on our great economic capacity and the fundamental appeal of our democratic system. It is time to shift the competition with our adversary from missiles and warheads to food and freedom—the weapons of peace.

Certain risks are required today to help free the world from bondage to nuclear deterrence and the risk of nuclear war. . . . Free people must always pay a proportionate price and run some risks—responsibly—to preserve freedom.

—Pastoral Letter
U.S. Catholic Bishops
1983

Words like disaster and catastrophe are too frivolous for the events that would inevitably follow a war with thermonuclear weapons. Damage is not the real term; the language has no word for it. Some people might survive, but survival is itself the wrong word. As to the thought processes of the people in high perches of government who believe that they can hide themselves underground somewhere (they probably can) and emerge later on to take over again the running of society (they cannot, in the death of society), or, more ludicrous, the underground headquarters already installed in the mountains for corporate executives who plan to come deranged out of their tunnels to reorganize the telephone lines or see to the oil business, these people cannot have thought at all.

—Lewis Thomas
Scientist

EIGHT

The Way Out:
The First Steps

IF THE UNITED STATES were to pursue nonmilitary competition with the Soviet Union, we would surely be the winner. To pursue the promise of rich rewards that would result from shifting to nonmilitary competition, we must first find a way out of our present unworkable course. To prove our country's leadership and to preserve our national security, it is we who must lead the way out of a nuclear weapons race that constantly grows more costly and dangerous. But where do we begin?

When a business policy is not producing the results intended, the first step is to stop doing what does not work. A prime example of this prudent practice is the Ford Motor Company's experience with the Edsel automobile. The experts who conceived and designed the Edsel were human beings who guessed wrong. If the company's decisions and budget had been controlled by Edsel ideologues—passionate believers in their brainchild—they might have continued to pour good money after bad and compounded a miscalculation into the death of a great corporation. But instead, they were objective and flexible. They recognized and admitted a mistake. They absorbed a huge financial loss in the short term, but in the long run, they took their company to an even brighter future.

This kind of crossroad decision, much magnified, confronts us today. We are shareholders in the American enterprise, and our Edsel is a national security policy that relies too heavily on nuclear weapons and military competition with the Soviet Union. As we have seen, it is a policy that, if continued, will almost certainly take us to a final bankruptcy from which we can never recover.

To avoid this catastrophe, we must stop doing what does not work. The unprecedented destructiveness of nuclear devices makes it impossible to rely any longer on the prenuclear notion that more weapons will make us safer. There are fifty thousand nuclear weapons in the world today. Even if we could protect ourselves against 98 percent of them, the remaining 2 percent could utterly devastate our country and the Soviet Union in a matter of hours.

Since more of these devices reduce rather than increase our security, sound business strategy calls for an alternative approach. We can no longer consider the nuclear arms race to be an unfortunate fact of life. We must be as objective, pragmatic, flexible, and as unafraid of change as the decision-makers who simply stopped making the Edsel. In order to save our national enterprise, and indeed ourselves and everything we value, we must see to it that the politicians—whose employers are the American people—stop and reverse the nuclear arms race.

There is no doubt that ending the nuclear arms race is one of the most difficult problems humanity has ever faced. There are no easy solutions, no panaceas for reversing the technological, bureaucratic, and ideological momentum whose inexorable force seems to be beyond control.

Over the coming decade, if current military plans are implemented, the United States will manufacture an average of five nuclear weapons every day. Pentagon plans call for building seventeen thousand new, more destructive devices, while retiring eleven thousand older, less efficient ones. Undoubt-edly, the Russians will again follow suit. Present arms control proposals would have little if any impact on the planned ex-pansion of nuclear arsenals. And now it seems we are on the verge of extending the territory of the arms race into outer space.

Attempts to arrive at arms control agreements continue, but in the present atmosphere of mutual distrust and hos-tility, the negotiations are slow, complex, and tedious. They offer little hope for reversing a process that has continued for nearly forty years. Indeed, current arms control negotiations have the eerie quality of an argument over the arrangement of the deck chairs aboard the *Titanic*.

Clearly, we are at an impasse. It is obvious that both sides must change. What is not so obvious is that it is within the power and tradition of the United States to lead the way out. Despite the changes that have occurred in the world situa-tion, the United States is still the strongest power on earth. This country is in a unique position to exercise leadership that can break the impasse and reduce the danger of nuclear holocaust.

There are compelling reasons why the United States should seize the initiative in calling a halt to a form of com-petition that reduces our security and does deep damage to our economy. The first and foremost is simply that we want to survive. So do the Russians, but it is unlikely that the Russian people can generate the initiative for change. The Soviet Union is a closed and autocratic society. Its citizens are de-nied the opportunity to affect their government's policies through the expression of popular will. Their system is a bu-reaucratic brontosaurus, designed to perpetuate the power of the Communist-party elite. The Soviet military sector com-mands the major share of the nation's productivity as well as a disproportionate amount of political power. We can hardly expect that such a regime will assume leadership in ending the arms race. Who, then, but the United States can lead the way?

Another reason why leadership is incumbent upon the United States is that we have led the way in the continuing acceleration of the arms race. The Soviets have followed our lead, continually matching the weapons and systems that were initiated by us. Most nuclear scientists agree that the United States has, in almost every instance, been first with technical innovations and new weapons systems, a situation that has led former M.I.T. president and Presidential Science Adviser Jerome Wiesner to comment that "we have been in an arms race with ourselves."

Dr. Herbert York (an eminent nuclear physicist who worked on the development of the first atomic bomb, was director of Defense Research and Engineering for the Defense Department, and served as science adviser to President Eisenhower) has stated unequivocally that the United States has been responsible for setting the rate and scale of the nuclear weapons competition.

> Over the last thirty years we have repeatedly taken unilateral actions that have unnecessarily accelerated the race. These actions have led to the accumulation of unnecessarily large numbers of oversized weapons. In short, these actions have led to the present situation of gross overkill. . . . Just as our unilateral actions were in large part responsible for the current dangerous state of affairs, we must expect that unilateral moves on our part will be necessary if we are ever to get the whole process reversed.

According to Dr. York, the United States can determine whether we move in the direction of further escalation or in the direction of effective arms control and reduction. American leadership is crucial now because time is running out. Weapons development is occurring at such a rapid pace that it is unlikely that even intensified arms negotiations could keep up. What could be achieved now may be impossible to accomplish in the very near future. With regard to reductions, it may well be a simple matter of now or never.

Another timely factor calling for U.S. action is the fact that both superpowers have achieved relative parity in nuclear forces and thus have the balance of power necessary for successful negotiations. The first principle of arms control in the nuclear age is that it achieve security for both sides. We cannot expect to "win" a negotiation, or as Gerard Smith, our SALT I negotiator, put it, "Strategic arms negotiations between equals may succeed or fail, but they are not won or lost."

The claims made by some that the Soviet Union has gained nuclear superiority over the United States are simply not true. In 1981, Secretary of Defense Harold Brown stated in his official report that "the United States and the Soviet Union are roughly equal in strategic nuclear power." A few months later, President Reagan's National Security Adviser Richard Allen stated that the U.S. and the U.S.S.R. are equal "in almost every meaningful measure of military power." At about the same time, Secretary of State Alexander Haig testified that "the United States is very, very strong and very, very capable, especially in the strategic area. Our systems are both more sophisticated and reliable and more technologically sound." Also in 1981, the Chairman of the Joint Chiefs of Staff stated, "I would not trade U.S. military capability overall for that of the Soviets."

It should be noted that there are differences in the way U.S. and Soviet weapons are deployed. U.S. strategic forces are based on the triad system—dispersed among land missiles, bomber forces, and submarines. The Soviet Union has deployed three fourths of its strategic weaponry in land-based missiles. The possibility that the Soviets could wipe out our land-based missiles in a first strike and leave us with no effective deterrent has now been shown to be at best a misguided fantasy and at worst a deliberate political ploy.

Now is the time for the United States to take *independent initiatives* that will break the arms control deadlock and accelerate the arms reduction process. As the leader of the free world and the leader in the nuclear weapons race, we should take action that is in our self-interest and made possible by our democratic system of government. We can demonstrate to the world our resourcefulness and imagination, our willingness to experiment and take a carefully calculated risk that is minimal when compared to the enormous risk of nuclear war.

There is a powerful precedent for this kind of leadership and American independent action. Twenty years ago President John F. Kennedy, speaking at the American University commencement, made the bold declaration that the United States would not conduct any further atmospheric nuclear testing as long as other nations would also refrain from testing. He described his action as a pledge to "make clear our good faith and solemn conviction on the matter." President Kennedy's independent initiative received a positive response from Premier Khrushchev, who then proposed a test ban that eventually formed the basis for the U.S.–U.S.S.R. Limited Test Ban Treaty of 1963. The treaty, which banned atmospheric, underwater, and outer-space nuclear tests, was also followed by the two superpowers' removal of ten thousand troops from Central Europe and cuts in production of nuclear weapons material.

Once again it is time for the United States to exercise leadership and take bold action. **We should begin immediately a step-by-step program of American initiatives aimed at slowing, stopping, and reversing the Soviet–American nuclear arms race.** This incremental program—a building-block approach to halting the arms race—would include the following steps:

STEP ONE: The United States would announce that we will suspend any further testing of nuclear weapons and challenge the Soviet Union to reciprocate while we conclude the negotiation of a formal Comprehensive Test Ban Treaty. If the Soviets continued testing or refused to conclude the Treaty within a reasonable period of time, the U.S. would no longer be bound to its proposal.

A Comprehensive Test Ban Treaty has been in negotiation since 1963, but the nuclear weapons establishment—a loose network of scientists, military men, nuclear war planners, and some members of Congress—has lobbied actively and successfully to block any agreement to suspend testing. President Reagan formally abandoned all efforts to negotiate the treaty in 1982.

Over the past twenty-four years, the issue of verification has been a major stumbling block in concluding a treaty. Although it is much easier to detect atmospheric testing, there have been significant advances in the ability to monitor underground tests as well. Independent scientific researchers have reported that "the technical capabilities needed to police a comprehensive test ban down to explosions of very small size unquestionably exist." There is the risk, of course, that small violations might go undetected, but these small risks must be weighed against the very positive advantage of taking a mutual step that could lead us out of the Soviet–American nuclear weapons impasse.

A moratorium on nuclear testing would be a realistic and quickly achievable first step in U.S. independent initiatives. A positive response by the Soviet Union would create a climate in which we could finally reach agreement on the long-sought Comprehensive Test Ban Treaty. Former Director of the Arms Control and Disarmament Agency Paul Warnke stated in June of 1983 that negotiations on the Comprehensive Test Ban were so close to completion that, if the United States and the Soviet Union were both willing, the Treaty could be signed within a period of thirty days.

If an American President were unwilling to propose such a moratorium on weapons testing, the Congress could take the initiative by amending the relevant appropriations bill or by other legislative action. Provision would be made, of course, for resumption of U.S. testing if Soviet tests continued. This first step is a no-risk, high-yield approach that—contingent upon Soviet response—could produce a significant breakthrough. We have nothing to lose and everything to gain.

STEP TWO: After accomplishing the critical first step of a test-ban agreement, we would have established some degree of mutual confidence along with procedures that would make successive steps less risky and less difficult. Our next independent initiative could be to propose a moratorium on the flight-testing of nuclear weapons delivery systems. Like the ban on testing, this step would be relatively easy to verify, since flight-testing of missiles and aircraft is highly visible.

Such a moratorium, again contingent upon Soviet compliance, would prevent the testing and thus inhibit the deployment of highly destabilizing delivery systems like the new family of ICBMs—our MX missile and whatever the Soviets will come up with as its counterpart. It would also inhibit deployment of the cruise missile as well as a whole new generation of very accurate sea-launched weapons.

As with each step of this proposal, a successful moratorium would be codified into formal agreements that would build confidence on both sides. Each would gradually strengthen its belief that the other was not adding to its nuclear capabilities.

STEP THREE: Building on the momentum of this sequential, incremental process, the United States should propose yet another moratorium on the deployment of any new nuclear weapons systems. As with testing, verification of this step is not difficult, since even now we are able to count every Soviet missile launcher, bomber, and submarine. Again, we would announce our own halt in deployment, challenging the Russians to do the same. In negotiating a formal agreement, we should also seek to make certain that both sides maintain their commitment to already agreed SALT I and II limits on the deployment of existing weapons systems.

STEP FOUR: With the first three steps successfully taken, we could then begin to face the far more difficult issue of banning the production of fissionable material and the actual production of nuclear warheads. Stopping production is more difficult to verify, since the manufacturing process is easier to conceal. But with the first three steps accomplished, there would be little motivation to continue making the weapons. It is also likely that there will be further advances in verification procedures. We should keep in mind that the Soviets have already formally accepted the principle of on-site inspection for arms control verification as part of a comprehensive test ban. The first three steps certainly would establish still more mutual confidence, a greater degree of trust, and implementation of improved verification procedures by both sides.

Stopping the production of new nuclear weapons offers several advantages to both sides: 1) It would stop the production of an entire generation of new weapons, now in development, which are dangerous and destabilizing; 2) It would prevent both sides from deploying additional cruise missiles that, because they are small and easily concealed, would make future arms control verification difficult, if not impossible; 3) It would keep the arms race from moving into outer space; and 4) Each side would still retain an effective nuclear deterrent capacity.

Impartial experts (among them, William Colby, former Director of the Central Intelligence Agency, Jeremy Stone,

Director of the American Federation of Scientists, and former CIA Deputy Director Herbert Scoville, now president of the Arms Control Association) agree that a halt in production is at least as verifiable as other arms agreements, if not more so, since it is much more difficult to verify complex numerical ceilings on various types of weapons than it is to detect evidence of significant weapons production. In testimony before Congress, former CIA Director Colby stated that "any program which offered the prospect of strategic advantage to the Soviets by definition would have to be of a size and consequent visibility that we could identify it long before it became a direct threat, and take defensive action against it."

In essence, Steps One, Two, Three, and Four of this proposal amount to an incremental nuclear weapons freeze—a step-by-step process for accomplishing the aims now set forth in the 1982 Bilateral Nuclear Weapons Freeze Initiative—a simple, straightforward proposal calling for an immediate halt to testing, production, and deployment of nuclear weapons by the United States and the Soviet Union. The freeze was supported by more than twelve million voters in nine states. It has been described as the largest referendum on a single issue in the history of the United States, and citizen support for its commonsense clarity continues to grow. Six months after the 1982 election results, a national poll showed that 79 percent of Americans favored the freeze. Its bipartisan support was demonstrated by the fact that 72 percent of the Republicans polled favored the freeze. Even the noted conservative columnist James Kilpatrick has stated that "there is nothing in the freeze resolution that a good conservative could not support."

The step-by-step approach proposed here, beginning with the moratorium on testing, could accomplish the aims of the widely favored Soviet–American freeze without necessitating lengthy and tedious negotiation of every aspect all in one lump. The most pressing need is to begin immediately the process of slowing, stopping, and reversing a nuclear arms race that continues to escalate.

STEP FIVE: Once the United States and the Soviet Union agree to halt future weapons development and to ensure that neither side could get ahead in weaponry, the ground would be laid for true reductions in the massive nuclear arsenals of both nations. Step Five in the process proposed here would begin with an appraisal of existing arsenals and the proposal of positive measures to carry out a stable, orderly, and balanced program of reductions. Each side would keep an adequate deterrent capability while lowering the level of its nuclear arsenal.

Former Ambassador to the Soviet Union George Kennan has made a proposal for massive reductions that is sensible, simple, and gets right to the heart of the matter. Kennan proposes an immediate, across-the-board 50-percent reduction in the nuclear arsenals of both superpowers, "to be implemented at once without further wrangling among the experts." The 50 percent left on each side would still be far more than enough to devastate the adversary.

Admiral Noel Gayler, former Director of the National Security Agency, has expanded upon Ambassador Kennan's proposal, suggesting practical ways it might be carried out. He believes that deep cuts of this nature are entirely feasible, that each side could simply turn in (to a joint U.S.–Soviet commission or an impartial third party) an equal number of nuclear devices. "Let each side choose the weapons it wishes to turn in, whether missile warheads, bombs or artillery shells. Each weapon would count the same—as one device. . . . A nuclear device is uniquely identifiable and can be counted without error when turned in; thus, there is full verification without intrusive inspection in either country."

Admiral Gayler's suggestion is to have the process begin with a small number of weapons—say, fifty—to test the method and develop confidence, and then continue on an agreed schedule toward very large reductions of perhaps ten thousand devices from each side. Both countries would still retain a small number of strategic weapons in reserve. Again, the risks involved are far outweighed by the immense risk of continuing to increase the destructive capability of arsenals that are already obscenely excessive.

This step-by-step program of American initiatives—the proposal of a moratorium first on weapons testing, then on testing of delivery systems, then on deployment and production, and finally the proposal of massive cuts in nuclear arsenals—represents a methodical process for breaking the momentum of the nuclear arms race with no real risk to our national security. In each step, our country could take independent action that would demonstrate good faith and give the Soviets an opportunity to demonstrate theirs as well. Independent initiatives by the United States are a pragmatic, incremental approach to a problem that too many of us have seen as having no solution. Such incrementalism is the essence of sound business practice, with each stage forming a solid basis for the following one. Step by step, our country can lead the way out.

If the United States were to lead the way, would the Soviet Union follow us? There is growing evidence that Soviet leadership desires serious negotiations to reduce the growing threat of annihilation and the crushing burden of the arms race. The Soviet economy, far less efficient and productive than that of the United States, has a host of economic problems—including failing agriculture, a shrinking work force, shortages of consumer goods, and backward technology—that plague the Soviet system. Increasing trouble with Russia's ethnic minorities, unrest in Poland, and a continuing war in Afghanistan add to problems the Soviet leadership cannot ignore. Reducing the drain of the arms race on their economy would enable the USSR to focus on serious domestic problems and perhaps curb its appetite for international adventurism.

As is the case with any competitor, it is unrealistic to expect the Soviets to act in our interest. But it is perfectly realistic to expect them to act in their own self-interest, if given the opportunity. Reversing the nuclear arms race is as much in their interest as it is in ours.

There are those who believe that we should continue the arms race precisely because it puts pressure on the Soviet system. But this point of view can only lead us down a very dangerous track. However repugnant the Soviet government is to us, we must accept the fact that it is here to stay. We must concede unequivocally to the Soviets their equal status as a superpower with legitimate security needs of their own. Our continuing threats only serve to increase Russian paranoia about American intentions and thus decrease our own security.

Much could be gained if we would realize that in a thermonuclear era what is good for the Russians is not necessarily bad for us or vice versa. We have powerful mutual interests, not the least of which is preventing a nuclear war which could wipe out both nations. Our own security is now directly dependent on the security of the Soviet Union. Their security, in turn, depends upon our own. We also have in common the need to stop the proliferation of nuclear weapons that could make us both hostage to smaller nations or to groups of terrorists. Addressing our common interests is not an idealistic notion, but a realistic response to our relationship at a point in history that presents a clear choice between co-existence and co-extermination.

Thus, as we seek negotiated arms agreements with the Soviet Union, we also need to find ways to facilitate the prospects for peaceful coexistence. Even if we have far fewer nuclear weapons, we will not reduce the danger of nuclear war until we reduce the fear, suspicion, and hostility on both sides. There is much that we can contribute to building a stable relationship with the Soviet Union. Initiatives on our part need not imply acceptance of Soviet policies or actions. Without abandoning the competition between the two countries, we can nevertheless seek to increase communication and cooperation with the Russian people and their government.

But we cannot afford to wait for improved U.S.–Soviet relations to begin reducing the threat of nuclear war. Nuclear weapons may be only the symptoms of Russophobia, but they are symptoms that can kill us. To survive, we must act now.

The series of first steps suggested here for independent American initiatives to break the nuclear impasse is not meant to be a detailed blueprint for action. Rather, it is an example of one practical alternative to the continuation of a counterproductive policy that could lead to the final bankruptcy of the American enterprise. What we need now are other straightforward proposals that can cut through the confusion and complexity which make the problem seem insurmountable. It is nonsense to insist that resolving the nuclear arms dilemma should be left to the experts. The experts are, after all, the ones who created the policy that brought us to the present point of potentially terminal peril. The myth of expertise is exactly that—a myth. It takes scientific skills to make a hydrogen bomb. It takes only common sense to know when there are too many hydrogen bombs. And common sense is precisely what is needed now.

Fortunately, the American people have begun to develop a clear view of this problem. Their common sense largely explains the growing majority who reject the traditional, ineffective approach to arms control, an approach that permits each side to build new weapons while talking about limits on older systems. The remarkably widespread bipartisan support for an immediate Soviet–American nuclear weapons freeze shows how clearly people have begun to see that we will never reduce nuclear weapons if both sides continue to build them at record rates—as they have done despite all previous traditional negotiating procedures. Only when production is fully frozen by both sides will the stage be set for an orderly program of real reductions, the ultimate goal of the nuclear weapons freeze favored by so large a percentage of the American people.

The basic issue is simple: Stop making the Edsel. Some will claim that there is no solution other than the course we have followed: Build more weapons. A senior officer of Ford Motor Company during the Edsel crisis told me there were those who argued that too much had been invested in the Edsel to stop production, that the company should stay the course. Had they prevailed, the result would have been bankruptcy. There are always people who say the risks of change are too great, but what greater risk could we face than the annihilation of all that we have worked for, the accumulation of thousands of years of human endeavor?

Business people who succeed know that when the survival of their enterprise is threatened, they must change course. As influential shareholders in our national enterprise, business leaders must mandate our management—our employees in government—to stop and reverse the nuclear arms race. We must tell them: Find a way. Come up with a plan. It can be done and it must be done. Do it.

Our unequivocal mandate for change is essential to slow, stop, and reverse the nuclear arms race.

I think that people want peace so much that one of these days governments had better get out of their way and let them have it.

—PRESIDENT DWIGHT D.
EISENHOWER
1959

Let us examine our attitude toward peace itself. Too many of us think it is impossible. Too many of us think it unreal. But that is a dangerous, defeatist belief. It leads to the conclusion that war is inevitable—that mankind is doomed—that we are gripped by forces we cannot control.

We need not accept this view. Our problems are manmade—therefore, they can be solved by man. And man can be as big as he wants. No problem of human destiny is beyond human beings. Man's reason and spirit have often solved the seemingly unsolvable—and we believe that they can do it again.

—PRESIDENT JOHN F.
KENNEDY
American University, 1963

Because everything we do and everything we are is in jeopardy, and because the peril is immediate and unremitting, every person is the right person to act and every moment is the right moment to begin, starting with the present moment.

—JONATHAN SCHELL
The Fate of the Earth

NINE

Preventing Nuclear War Is Your Business

OUR NATIONAL ENTERPRISE is committed to an unwinnable nuclear arms race—an unworkable, dangerous, and possibly terminal policy. The reasons given for continuing this policy are based on outdated or inaccurate assumptions and a failure to recognize the new realities of the nuclear age. The situation is further complicated by rigid and inflexible attitudes—a closed-mindedness that precludes the possibility of fresh, pragmatic thinking that could yield workable alternative approaches.

The forces that perpetuate the nuclear arms race—momentum, competitor obsession, and the assumption of inevitability—are exactly opposite to what makes for the continued vitality and success of a business enterprise.

Bureaucratic, technological, and ideological momentum have infused the nuclear juggernaut with a life of its own, making it a creature independent of its creators and of its keepers. What business could survive in the long run if it allowed institutional momentum to determine company policy?

A major force threatening our national enterprise is com-

petitor obsession—our Russophobia. The fear of under-
estimating our major competitor drives us to overestimate
intentions and capabilities: What the Soviets might do becomes more important than what they actually can do, and
blinds us to what we should do. The worst-case fantasies of
our military planners induce an escalation of weapons that the
other side's fantasizers are then compelled to match.

Competitor obsession has caused us to blame communism
for all human ills. The challenge of communism should not be
taken lightly. It should be confronted, however, with balanced businesslike judgment, not with paranoid hysteria. We
have been spending our skills and our economic substance to
guard our gates against an adversary who has nothing to gain
from attacking us except his own destruction. Our nation has
come to resemble a person so obsessed with fear of catastrophe that he spends his fortune on insurance against unlikely
events while his family starves and his house falls apart.

Our competitor obsession is a self-destructive compulsion,
keeping us from the most important business of all—preserv-
ing and improving our own national plant, and marketing our
unique products, food and freedom.

Another force that perpetuates the nuclear weapons race
is inevitability—the unquestioned assumption that we have
no choice, that there is nothing else we can do. We have come
to accept the nuclear weapons race as an unchangeable fact of
life. We act as though forces outside our control keep us from
pursuing any other course. "After all," we tell ourselves, "if
there were an alternative to the arms race, surely the experts
would have come up with it by now. What can we do?"

The assumption of inevitability is dangerously debilitating. It anesthetizes the most powerful voice in a democracy:
its people. We would do well to remember that democracy
assures one thing only: that its people get exactly what they
deserve. In the final analysis, our government does what we

as citizens want done. If the people will lead, in time, the leaders will follow.

The most important changes in the history of our country have come in response to the will of the people. Slavery, for example, was considered for centuries to be an inevitable part of the human condition and an economic necessity in our own country. It was finally abolished in response to years of public pressure from a steadily growing number of Americans who became convinced that if our democratic system did not abolish slavery, slavery would, in effect, abolish democracy.

Other examples of effective public pressure for change include child-labor reform and the expansion of civil rights for minorities and women. The Vietnam War was at long last brought to an end only because enough American citizens came to feel that it was a war that made no sense. Our history provides ample evidence that those we elect to govern do respond to the will of the people once that will presses its way up through the body politic.

We have never faced a more important problem than the growing danger of nuclear war. We are quickly running out of time. Nuclear holocaust becomes more probable every day. In fact, distinguished scientists, diplomats, and even retired military officers consider nuclear war inevitable before the year 2000 unless we change our direction now.

You and I would never sit by and watch our own business enterprise slide into disaster. We would act. Even the slightest possibility that our company might fail within a few years would prompt us to reassess basic assumptions, discard potentially disastrous policies, and look for workable alternatives. As business people, we learn to understand that we benefit by recognizing a mistaken commitment and changing direction. Mistakes are forgivable. What is unforgivable—for countries as well as corporations—is continuing on a losing course, especially when that course could prove suicidal.

The decision-makers of our national enterprise are not madmen bent on destruction. They are sincere and dedicated people who have pursued a mistaken course. But our country is not the private possession of people elected to office. It is our country, too. And since those who work for us in government have failed to be objective and flexible, it is we who must act to press upon them the need for policies that fit the realities of a nuclear age.

There have been times when a few people have changed the course of human history. A little over two hundred years ago, a relative handful of American colonists—most of them businessmen and entrepreneurs—rallied others behind the idea that gave birth to our nation.

Today, a similar opportunity exists for business executives and entrepreneurs to join with others at the leading edge of change, to become a visible force of active leadership in preventing the death of our nation.

Business people are a central component of our nation's economic life. Ours is a voice that our fellow citizens will not ignore, a voice that our policymakers cannot dismiss. It is my conviction that by speaking out with clarity and courage we can persuade our people and our government that—just as in any bad business deal—there is always a way out.

I am aware that traditionally, business leaders have avoided taking stands on controversial political issues. Corporate responsibility—the idea that a firm's obligations extend to the general welfare rather than being limited to providing a service or product and making a profit—is a relatively recent development. Beginning in the 1950's as a self-serving and defensive tactic to mollify public opinion, corporate responsibility evolved into what was, in the early 1960's, an essentially good-guy posture: passive, nonpolitical, noncontroversial, and still largely directed toward creating a favorable image.

Then came the Vietnam War. The concept of corporate responsibility was lifted to a new level, as business leaders, often painfully and with a great deal of soul-searching, began to redefine their self-interest to include their society as well as their businesses. Corporate executives, venture capitalists, officers, managers, and entrepreneurs began to become involved in the search for peace. They became social innovators, active citizens on the cutting edge of a controversial problem.

As more and more business leaders realized the need to end a mistaken and self-damaging war, articles and advertisements began to appear in business journals, and letters on corporate stationery landed on White House, Pentagon, and congressional desks. While other sectors of society certainly had an important impact on government policy, it was the weight of business authority as much as anything that helped tip the balance, to turn the question from "How soon will we win this holy war?" to "How soon can we extricate ourselves from this unholy mess?"

In time this new kind of corporate responsibility extended to the very top tier of American business when men like then IBM board chairman Thomas J. Watson and Louis B. Lundborg, chairman of the board of the Bank of America, the world's largest private bank, spoke out boldly against the war. Louis Lundborg testified before the Senate Foreign Relations Committee that regardless of who was responsible for the war, "the rest of us have gone along pretty supinely. If anyone is to blame," Mr. Lundborg continued, "it is people like me for not speaking up and not speaking out sooner—for not asking, 'What goes on here?'"

But unlike the turmoil and turbulence surrounding Vietnam, the nuclear weapons issue seems quiet, almost serene. There are no campus riots, no body counts, no atrocity stories, no napalmed villages on the evening news. Nothing to move us to outrage. Just the relentless tick of the Doomsday clock as it moves ever closer to the moment none of us wants to think about. But if we are to survive, we must not only think, we must act. And we must act now. As Walter Cronkite has said, "It is not pleasant to look death in the face. But unless we do, we are doomed."

A New York financier recently told me, "I've never been vocal about, or in any way involved in, political and social issues. I always thought it best for businessmen to leave that to others. But now I realize that the need to stop and reverse the nuclear arms race is no more political than the need to find a cure for cancer. So I want to stop hiding in my office. I'd like your help in finding ways to get other businessmen—including *Fortune*'s top five hundred—to break their traditional silence. Because of what the nuclear weapons race is doing to our nation, and what it threatens to do to everything we value, they have nothing to gain—and everything to lose—from continued silence."

Thomas J. Watson, chairman emeritus of IBM Corporation and former Ambassador to the Soviet Union, has said,

Those who play sandbox games with nuclear weapons are either allowing slick technology to blind them to reality or they still nourish a belief that we can bully or spend the Soviet Union into submission, and, failing that, we can fight and win a nuclear war. Intentionally or not, they are leading us toward disaster.

This is a critical moment for American democracy. Americans in great number are listening to their own common sense. They are beginning to see through the smokescreens created by misuse of technical expertise. . . . They are on the verge of recapturing their destiny from technology and from political manipulation. They had better hurry.

Other respected and influential executives are also breaking their silence and taking a stand, voicing their concern about the direction and danger of our national security policy. They include: Lewis Branscomb, IBM vice-president and chief scientist; Lawrence Huntington, chief executive officer of Fiduciary Trust of New York; Donald Kendall, chairman of PepsiCo; Gloria Lemos, vice-president of the Coca-Cola Company; Robert Schmidt, vice-chairman of Control Data Corp; and C. William Verity, chairman of ARMCO, Inc., and former president of the U.S. Chamber of Commerce and head of President Reagan's Task Force on Private Sector Initiatives.

The list is impressive and growing. But it is not nearly long enough; the voice of business is not nearly loud enough. If a substantial segment of the business community responds to this great challenge by speaking out, we can stop and reverse our headlong race toward the final bankruptcy.

What then, you may ask, as an individual, as a business person, can you do? The best place to begin is to ask yourself that same question: What can I do? Your answer depends on your particular interests, resources, and business relationships—on who you are and whom you know. Perhaps you can start by talking informally with your business associates. Tell them of your concern, remind them of what is at stake, and let them know just how vital their participation is. Then, give them a copy of this briefing and invite them to join you in speaking out and taking action.

Communicate your views to local and national leaders. If you can't visit a person, call on the telephone, or write a letter. Even if you've never been involved in politics, as a business person you possess considerable influence in Washington. This point was brought home to me recently during a visit to the office of a Congressman who showed me how his large volume of mail was sorted and distributed. Most of the incoming letters were handled by aides. Letters on business stationery, however, came directly to him.

THE TRIMTAB FACTOR

Make your concern known in your local community. Let people know that, as a business person, as a neighbor, as a citizen, and as a human being, you are deeply concerned about where the nuclear arms race is taking us and what it is doing to our nation. If you will but look around, you will discover that you are sitting in the middle of an unprecedented groundswell of growing public concern. People everywhere are waking up to the peril we are living in, and they are getting involved. A vast network of citizens from all walks of life is emerging in every part of the country—probably right in your own community. Step forward; make yourself known; speak out.

This is no time to mince words. You are the crucial element—the trimtab factor. What you do—or fail to do—at this critical moment in human history will determine not merely the shape of the future, but whether there will be a future at all.

Dig a hole, cover it with a couple of doors and then throw three feet of dirt on top. . . . It's the dirt that does it . . . if there are enough shovels to go around, everybody's going to make it.

—T. K. Jones
Deputy Undersecretary of
Defense for Strategic and
Theater Nuclear Forces

Early in my business career, I was given a guideline that has served me well in my personal enterprises and as a member of various corporate boards: **Never bet the whole company.** If we had two identical earths, perhaps gambling with the survival of one might be considered an affordable risk. But since we have only one, is it a good business risk to allow mortal (and therefore possibly mistaken) bureaucrats to bet our whole company?

—Harold Willens

TEN

Case Study of a Corporate Turnaround

MEANWHILE, in the town nestled at the foot of the mountain, life went on much as it always had. The townspeople didn't give much thought to the growing danger of a catastrophic avalanche because they thought there was nothing they could do about it. It was, after all, a regrettable but necessary evil, and thinking about it would only leave them frightened and depressed. So they pursued their own lives, took care of their families, and planned for the future, hoping that the management of the two corporations and their security experts would prevent an avalanche, just as they always had.

But as time went on, the competition between USA, Inc. and USSR, Inc. grew more bitter, and the condition of the town deteriorated even further. Despite the confident assurances of the Public Relations Department, many of the townspeople who were stockholders in USA, Inc. began to have the uneasy feeling that something was terribly wrong. Suddenly, the idea of leaving the future of their businesses, their families, and the entire town in the hands of security experts didn't seem like such a smart thing to do.

Some of the USA, Inc. stockholders decided to investigate the avalanche danger on their own. What they discovered horrified them. The more they found out, the more anxious they became. Soon their anxiety gave way to anger. They demanded a shareholders' meeting to discuss the future of the company.

At the meeting, USA, Inc.'s management team listened politely as representatives of various shareholder groups came to the podium to present their concerns. A local doctor began by reporting on the findings by the medical community that even a small explosion on the mountain would result in a massive slide of snow, rocks, and earth that would bury a large portion of the town. The casualties sure to occur would overtax the town's limited medical facilities. A large-scale avalanche and landslide, he predicted, would be an unimaginable catastrophe. A scientist explained how both companies were developing computer systems to control the new generation of detonators on the mountain because of concern that human control was too slow. A teacher told how her students were becoming increasingly pessimistic and cynical, and how young children were having nightmares of being buried alive. A member of the town council, having been asked by the management of USA, Inc. to prepare plans for a mass evacuation in case of avalanche, told of reaching the appalling conclusion that such plans were ludicrous and impossible. Even members of the local clergy, who would normally not involve themselves in commercial matters, felt compelled to speak out about the morality of conducting business by threatening death and destruction.

But the most frightening prospect of all was described by a member of the board of realtors. Thus far, he said, only USA, Inc. and USSR, Inc. could afford to buy the very expensive mountain property on which to rig their explosives. But now, smaller companies—some of them unpredictable and unstable—wanted a piece of the action. They had begun negotiating the purchase of their own land on the mountain, thus establishing themselves as an avalanche threat as well.

When this last speaker left the podium, the Chief Executive Officer walked over to the microphone. "My dear

friends," he said warmly, "let me first thank you for your expression of deep concern about this very important issue. I
know that I speak for every member of the board—*your*
board of directors—when I say that we share your concern.
No one knows more about the dangers of an avalanche, and
we never forget that it is our responsibility to make sure that
such a catastrophe never occurs. Why, we'd like nothing better than to march on up to the top of the mountain right now
and dismantle every single one of our explosive devices, but,
as you well know, we can't. The threat posed by USSR, Inc.
makes that impossible.

"So, my friends, while your aims are well intentioned, you
simply don't understand the complexities of a situation that
can only be clear to the experts. The only way to stop the
avalanche threat is to make more, not fewer, explosives. We
need to prove to our competition that we mean business. This
will force them to take meaningful steps to reduce their explosives. Only then will we be able to see the day when our town
is a safe and prosperous place for everyone. So if there is nothing more on the agenda, I'd like to close this meeting by—"

Suddenly, a loud voice came from the back of the room.
"Just one minute, please. There is still one group that is yet to
be heard from."

All eyes turned to a well-dressed, distinguished-looking
man as he made his way down the aisle and up to the podium.
After adjusting the microphone, he turned to the board of
directors and began.

"Thus far, you've heard physicians appeal to your reverence for life, scientists appeal to your fear, clergymen appeal
to your conscience. I am here to appeal to your common sense
and to mention some economic realities.

"I'm here as a shareholder in this enterprise and as a businessman. As president of the local chamber of commerce, I
represent the members of the business community. In that
role, it is my responsibility to tell you that the operating pol-

icy of this company is not merely ill-advised, it is the ultimate in bad business."

The members of the board looked at each other. This was not what they had expected. They all leaned forward in their chairs.

"I realize," said the Chief Executive, "that you and your business colleagues are not the kind of people to make rash judgments or irresponsible accusations, but those are very strong words. On what grounds can you say these things; what are your facts?"

The businessman asked for a chart to be brought to the front of the room. "Just take a look at this organization's performance indicators over the long term: gross sales, down; net profits, down; productivity, never lower; budget deficit, never higher; share of market, deteriorating rapidly; corporate image, at its lowest; employee morale, pathetic. Nobody can argue with these figures."

"But wait a minute." A board member stood to speak. "This situation isn't our fault. Everyone knows that USSR, Inc. means to put us out of business. They are the ones who keep putting more explosives up on the mountain!"

The businessman turned to him. "Now let's be honest about this. We all know that this company was first to add guards and place explosives on the mountain. Why, we've made all the advances in security devices, with USSR, Inc. following our lead. They're afraid we're going to put them out of business!

"In fact, we've been using most of our resources in an effort to *stop* the competition. They, in turn, have been doing everything they can to *stop* us from stopping them. As a result, the market potential has been severely damaged. The smaller enterprises are borrowing more and more money from the large companies in order to stay afloat, their employees are beginning to suffer, and their management has become unstable and subject to frequent change. As a result,

these organizations are now easy prey to the seductive promises of our competition.

"In such a market," he continued, "it is difficult to make
positive, forward-looking plans and act on them. We are too
busy reacting to our competitor and to unpredictable events.
This uncertainty increases our desire for security. So we do
the only thing we've ever done to make ourselves feel safer:
We spend more and more money on security devices. Now,
the danger of avalanche has become much greater than the
threat posed by USSR, Inc."

The shareholders applauded the businessman while the
board members looked uncomfortable. He continued, "I'm
afraid you have strayed from one of the basic tenets of sound
business practice—*never bet the whole company.* It's one
thing to direct some of our resources toward so-called security
against imaginary events that might happen. But it's quite another thing to risk destroying all of USA, Inc. as well as the
entire town. Your policymakers seem oblivious to the fact that
if those devices on the mountain are triggered, even accidentally, it will mean the end of everything we've worked for—
our companies, our families, even our lives."

The room was silent as the businessman paused for a moment. Then a board member spoke up with passion. "What
you don't understand, Mr. Businessman, is that we have no
choice! Why, USSR, Inc. is totally unscrupulous—"

"Hold on a minute," the businessman interrupted. "That
old argument will get us nowhere. We need some fresh thinking on this whole issue, and the members of the chamber of
commerce have some useful ideas. My colleagues and I are
convinced that without reducing corporate security, this company can adopt a positive marketing policy that will leave USSR,
Inc. in the dust! We have before us what may be the greatest
marketing opportunity in the history of this company."

"Opportunity?" The board members sat up straighter.
"What opportunity?"

"It's quite simple actually," the businessman continued. "We in the business community propose that USA, Inc. return to the original intention of the founders of this company: *Market the best product*. Why, our products have always set us apart from every other firm and made us very successful. If we'd just focus on what we have to offer rather than on hysterical concern for absurdly defined security, we'd be back on a healthy, profitable course in no time.

"The benefits to USA, Inc. are obvious: We would create friends, customers, and raw-material suppliers out of what are now resentful, dependent, and unstable companies, and at the same time reduce the appeal of our competitor's products. This would expand commerce in general and add stability to the marketplace. It would create a secure climate in which the entire town can grow and prosper."

"Now wait just a minute, Mr. Businessman," a voice interrupted. It was the chief of the Security Division. "You talk as if we're the only company involved in this competition. You seem to forget that there's a powerful organization out there whose entire operating philosophy is the antithesis of ours, whose management has stated publicly that it is their intention to put us out of business! We can't possibly stop the security race. That is, unless you're suggesting that we simply turn our back on the threat from USSR, Inc. dismantle our security devices, fire our guards, and just let them take over?"

"Absolutely not!" exclaimed the businessman. "Our choices are not merely between more explosives or removing them altogether. We at the chamber of commerce believe that USSR, Inc. wants out of this mess just as much as we do. I know for a fact they have serious financial problems. And common sense argues they don't want to die in an accidental or intentional avalanche any more than we do."

"Okay, then Mr. Businessman," said the security chief. "What's your plan?"

The businessman picked up some papers he'd brought

with him to the podium and passed them out to the board members. "My colleagues and I are proposing a series of steps this company could take that would enable both USA, Inc. and USSR, Inc. to stop our competition in security devices and gradually remove the explosives from the mountain. These are incremental steps on both sides that will not threaten the security of either. Of course this means taking some small calculated risks. But our security capability is strong enough to do that—and let's not forget that these small calculated risks would reduce the growing risk we now face of an avalanche that would end everything. USA, Inc. has always been the leading company in this town. It's time for us to assume leadership again, before it's too late."

"But this isn't a plan," the security chief objected, "this is just an outline. How do you propose to implement this?"

"That question," the businessman replied, "is exactly the one I pose to you, our management. Your so-called solution has become the problem—a potentially terminal problem for our company. We shareholders are the owners of this business. You are our employees. If we agree to this plan, then it's up to you to make it work. When you are prepared to make that commitment, I'm sure you'll find lots of ways to proceed. And, of course, the chamber of commerce would consider it a privilege to consult with you on the plan's implementation."

The Chief Executive Officer and the board members looked at each other, then the CEO broke the silence. "We'd like a little time to discuss this matter among ourselves. It looks like we've got some serious rethinking to do."

For the next several days, the board of directors met in closed-door executive session. During that time, they called upon the businessman and other consultants for advice. Within a week, the company officially and publicly announced that for a six-month period, it would not test a single security device. Then USA, Inc. waited to see if USSR, Inc. would follow suit. Since USSR, Inc. management had poor performance indicators of its own to worry about, it welcomed the chance to begin to reduce its security budget. This first step created a new climate for talks between the two companies to proceed in earnest.

Before very long, both companies had mutually agreed to suspend the manufacture of any additional security devices, and were beginning to talk seriously about how best to dismantle the existing ones. They were then in a good position to influence the small, unstable companies not to buy property on the mountain. When the townspeople realized that the security competition was actually slowing to a halt, and that the threat of an avalanche was greatly reduced, they were relieved and happy, and felt a new sense of respect for USA, Inc.

Meanwhile, USA, Inc. found many ways to reinvest the money it was saving. The company put additional funds into Research and Development to come up with new and improved products and production techniques and employed many additional people who desperately needed jobs. They also began to repair the physical facilities and to buy new, more sophisticated and efficient machinery and equipment.

Soon, USA, Inc.'s steadily climbing budget deficit leveled off and then started downward. In fact, all of the performance indicators began to turn in the right direction. Market research indicated that the management and employees of companies all over town had begun to perceive USA, Inc. as a forward-looking, innovative, and highly profitable enterprise, a model organization that ought to be emulated by other companies seeking the same kind of success. Employees and shareholders alike began to rediscover their almost-forgotten feeling of genuine pride and respect for their company.

Clear thinking and prudent initiatives had started USA, Inc. on a new road, one that could lead to a secure and prosperous future not only for the company, but for the entire town.

A Personal Note

On November 2, 1982, the California Bilateral Nuclear Weapons Freeze Initiative was approved by nearly four million voters in an election closely watched by the media in this country and other parts of the world. My phones immediately began to ring off the hook. As state chairman of the campaign, I was being interviewed by the press, thanked by co-workers, and congratulated by friends throughout the country.

Although I had devoted myself entirely to the freeze campaign for eighteen grueling months and raised several million dollars to run it effectively, it seemed inappropriate to accept the acknowledgment and praise. Hundreds of co-workers deserved it at least as much as I. Moreover, I had done nothing altruistic. In fact, I had never done anything more self-serving. I had worked for what I wanted most from life—the opportunity for myself, my wife, my children, my grandchildren, and other people I cared about to survive. I had not *given* time, effort, and money. I had *invested* in a venture that might help to prevent a nuclear holocaust that could mean the end of everyone I love and everything I own.

Every business executive I have ever known feels exactly as I do about those they love. I have often wondered how the men whose personal or company profits derive from the manufacture of nuclear bombs and missiles, some of whom I have come to know personally, can fail to make the connection between the weapons they are making and the growing danger of a nuclear war in which their children could be incinerated. To me, it seems they are reaping "the profits of doom."

I am reminded of a poignant story told to me by Averell Harriman, former Ambassador to the Soviet Union. During an evening he spent with then Soviet Premier Leonid Brezhnev, whom Harriman had known for years, the Russian leader pulled out his wallet, and like any proud grandpa, showed Harriman a picture of his first great-grandchild. After admiring the smiling face in the photograph, Harriman looked back at the Soviet premier to discover tears welling up in Mr. Brezhnev's eyes. "This child should be a source of great joy," Harriman exclaimed. "Why do you weep?" The Soviet leader responded sadly, "With what your government and my government are doing, what chance does this child have to live out its life?"

If anyone has great cause to "hate the Russians," I am that person. I was born in Russia and during my childhood experienced the terror of the Bolshevik Revolution. My recollections of life there still return in occasional nightmares. One such dream brings back memories of watching several drunken soldiers force their way into our tiny house and hearing them threaten to kill us all if we did not give them money and a few other things. In another periodic dream, I smell the smoke and stare with sickened sadness at the flames of nearby homes set afire by a band of marauders.

After my family and I escaped from Russia illegally in 1922 and arrived in the United States, what I had already experienced taught me to appreciate my newfound freedom with a passionate intensity that could only be felt by one who had lived in a land where liberty and law did not exist. I have always found it difficult to describe the depth of my devotion to the democratic system of this country. In my own mind, I have sometimes compared my feelings to those of a crippled person who suddenly, miraculously, regains the use of paralyzed limbs.

My emotional susceptibility to Russophobia is one thing. Common sense tells me that committing national and personal suicide is not the way to deal with an adversary. Moreover, recognition that change is inescapable causes me to feel that as younger Soviet leaders replace the old guard, they may be less paranoid and more attuned to the fact that economic problems matter more than ideological abstractions. The era of "isms" is as dead as the dinosaur, but no one seems to have noticed it. (Example: U.S.–China relationship.)

I have often wished that the leaders of both the United States and the Soviet Union could have witnessed what I saw in 1945 in Hiroshima and Nagasaki. Years later I had the opportunity to meet with both President Carter and President Reagan and to propose to them that they invite their Soviet counterpart to an informal summit meeting in Hiroshima. It remains my fervent hope that at some point the two men who can push the button could simply meet, man to man, human to human, in the city that witnessed the dawn of the nuclear age. Perhaps a nonagenda meeting there might produce the will to move our two nations away from the precipice of nuclear annihilation.

But in the very near future, we may need to worry less about the superpowers starting a nuclear war than about a war erupting from the proliferation of nuclear weapons—from hydrogen bombs in the hands of unstable dictators or fanatical terrorists. As part of the American delegation to the United Nations Special Session on Disarmament in 1978, I had occasion to hear representatives of Third World countries angrily denounce the U.S. and the U.S.S.R. for preaching nuclear abstention to others while practicing nuclear escalation themselves.

Although I was among those appointed by the Carter administration to represent the United States at this special UN session, I am not an advocate of disarmament. I consider disarmament to be a noble ideal, but a utopian fantasy given our present world situation. As we seek to stop and reverse the nuclear arms race, I understand the practical need to maintain an effective military capability that includes credible nuclear deterrence. Presently, however, the nuclear arsenals of both superpowers exceed any rational definition of deterrence.

One of the most important things business leaders can do is to ask the politicians and hard-sell technologists who work for us: What the hell do you mean by deterrence? Define it in language we can understand, or we'll hire others who can. Why do we need to pile up more overkill capability when we can already destroy our adversary many times over? Who's in charge here, anyway?

Only an informed and aroused public can stop the dangerous policy of adding more and more weapons to our already redundant nuclear arsenals. After two decades of despairing involvement I now feel a strong sense of hope that the recent groundswell of support for the Soviet–American freeze proposal marks the beginning of a massive citizen effort to end and reverse the nuclear arms race.

In such an effort business executives can play a vital role. Business people cannot be credibly labeled "Communist dupes" or "agents of the KGB." I recall how angry President Lyndon Johnson became in the 1960's when he learned about the Business Executives Move for Vietnam Peace, an organization of which I was cofounder and national cochairman. A friend who worked in the White House at the time told me how LBJ had fumed because business leaders simply aren't "soft-headed" or "soft on communism" (President Johnson's favorite charges against Americans who opposed our mistaken

Vietnam venture). The ending of the war in Vietnam came about, not by the desire of a President, but through the persistent efforts of many citizens. Respected analysts have publicly reported that the involvement of the business community in the opposition to that war was a crucial factor that turned Congress around.

Turning our ship of state away from a course that can lead to nuclear war is no small challenge, but the rewards of such an undertaking are great. If you see that your self-interest, your love for your children and grandchildren, leaves you no choice but to speak out, you will reap a personal reward beyond measure.

Many highly successful men and women in business have shared with me the feeling that all they had achieved was simply not enough. They knew there was something more. The past two decades have convinced me that this "something more" is the natural human desire to have an impact on the world about us, to strive to have our lives be of genuine consequence. In other words, when every other human need is met, the highest aspiration of all reveals itself—the desire to make a difference.

This issue provides such an opportunity. In fact, who in all of history has been faced with such an opportunity as this? We have the chance to apply our special capabilities and influence to the very preservation of the human enterprise, to play a vital role in ensuring the future of the human race.

It is not pleasant to look death in the face. But unless we do, we are doomed.

—**WALTER CRONKITE**
September 15, 1982

The only thing necessary for the triumph of evil is for good men to do nothing.

—**EDMUND BURKE, 1795**

Source Notes

CHAPTER TWO: The Trimtab Factor

Page 26: Albert Einstein quoted by Lincoln P. Bloomfield and Harland Cleveland in *Disarmament and the U.N. Strategy for the United States*, 1978.

Page 27: Concerning the trimtab effect, Buckminister Fuller once stated, "When I thought about steering the course of spaceship earth and all of humanity, I saw most people trying to turn the boat by pushing the bow around. I saw that by being all the way at the tail of the ship, by just kicking my foot to one side or the other, I could create the 'low pressure' which would turn the whole ship. If someone wanted to write my epitaph, I would want it to say 'Call me Trimtab.'" (*The Graduate Review*, March 1980.)

Page 29: Henry Kissinger was quoted by Elizabeth Drew in "An Argument over Survival," *The New Yorker*, April 4, 1977, page 104.

Page 29: President Reagan's statement was made in a press conference on January 19, 1981. Senator Proxmire's statement was made on the floor of the U.S. Senate in August 1980.

CHAPTER THREE: Origins of a Bad Business Policy

Pages 33–35: Some of the ideas discussed here were inspired by Archibald MacLeish, whose prophetic essay "The Conquest of America" first appeared in *Atlantic* magazine in 1949 and was reprinted in the March 1980 issue of *Atlantic* (page 35).

Pages 35–36: Senator Fulbright's quote is from his still very relevant book

Source Notes

Old Myths and New Realities (Random House, 1964). This statement appears on page 110.

Page 36: President Eisenhower's comments on the military industrial complex were made in his farewell address, January 16, 1961.

Pages 37–38: The notion that the United States is fighting the wrong battle with the wrong weapon is explored more fully in Sidney Lens's book *The Maginot Line Syndrome: America's Hopeless Foreign Policy* (Ballinger, 1983).

CHAPTER FOUR: A Competition No One Can Win

Pages 41–45: The information about the history of the nuclear arms race and our present level of nuclear weaponry derives from *Beyond the Freeze: The Road to Nuclear Sanity* by Daniel Ford, Henry Kendall, and Steven Nadis of the Union of Concerned Scientists (Beacon Press, 1982).

Pages 46–47: The information on "broken arrows" and accidental nuclear war comes from the Winter 1982 edition of the Physicians for Social Responsibility newsletter and from Chapter 1 of *Russian Roulette: The Superpower Game* by Arthur Macy Cox (Times Books, 1982).

Pages 47–48: For more information on horizontal proliferation, see Congressman Ed Markey's book *Nuclear Peril: The Politics of Proliferation* (Ballinger, 1982). The quote appears on page 131.

Page 50: Lord Mountbatten is quoted from an address he made in 1979.

CHAPTER FIVE: The Decline of America

Page 55: Regarding economists, see A. F. Ehrbar, "Stymied by the Deficit," *Fortune* magazine, November 15, 1982; "Guns vs. Butter," *Business Week*, November 29, 1982; and "Weidenbaum Faults Defense Budget Rises," *Baltimore Sun*, August 27, 1982.

Pages 56–57: For more information, see *The Political Economy of Arms Reduction: Reversing Economic Decay*, edited by Lloyd J. Dumas. Professor Dumas also assisted in the preparation of this chapter.

Page 57: Also useful in the preparation of this chapter was *The Freeze Economy*, edited by Dave McFadden and Jim Wake for the Economic Issues Task Force of the Nuclear Weapons Freeze Campaign and the Mid-Peninsula Conversion Project. Regarding R&D expenditures, see "Looting the Means of Production," *The New York Times*, July 26, 1981.

Source Notes

Page 58: The information about jobs comes from the 1982 edition of *The Empty Pork Barrel: Unemployment and the Pentagon Budget,* prepared by Marion Anderson of Employment Research Associates in Lansing, Michigan.

Page 59: The study by the Council on Economic Priorities is reported by Robert De Grasse, Jr., and David Gold in "Military Spending's Damage to the Economy," *The New York Times,* December 29, 1981.

CHAPTER SIX: A New Look at the Competition

Pages 72–74: Two views of the Soviet Union are presented in Ambassador Kennan's book *The Nuclear Delusion: Soviet-American Relations in the Atomic Age* (Pantheon, 1982).

Pages 75–78: Information in this chapter was drawn from *What About The Russians—and Nuclear War?,* published by Ground Zero (Pocket Books, 1983) and from the booklet "Questions and Answers on the Soviet Threat and National Security," published by the American Friends Service Committee.

Page 79: President Kennedy discussed U.S.–Soviet relations in his famous Commencement Address at American University in 1963.

Page 81: Robert F. Kennedy is quoted in Anthony Lewis's syndicated newspaper column "The Dreams Are Still Worth Dreaming," June 1983.

Page 81: John Naisbitt's book *Megatrends: Ten New Directions Transforming Our Lives* was published in 1982 by Warner Books.

CHAPTER SEVEN: Weapons of Peace

Page 85: Regarding economic opportunity in the Third World, see Chapter 3 of *Megatrends.*

Pages 85–86: Regarding Mexico, see "Why Support for IMF Is Crucial to U.S.," by Congressman Lee H. Hamilton, *San Francisco Chronicle,* May 11, 1983.

Page 86: Barbara Ward is quoted in *Megatrends,* page 76.

Pages 87–91: For more information on IFAD, see page 9 of Vol. 15 of *A Shift in the Wind,* a quarterly publication of The Hunger Project, San Francisco, California. The Hunger Project provided the information about world hunger on page 89 and information about Africa on page 90.

Source Notes

Page 91: David Lamb's article, "Is America the Root of Africa's Rebellion?," appeared in the *San Francisco Chronicle*, March 30, 1983.

Page 91: The *Wall Street Journal* article, "Whither Africa: The Continent's Poor Are Turning Westward for Aid but Not Allies," was written by June Kronholz and appeared on March 21, 1983.

Page 93: General Meyer was quoted in *The New York Times*, June 10, 1983.

Pages 93–94: Copies of the Report of the Presidential Commission on World Hunger are available for $6.00 from the Superintendent of Documents, U.S. Government Printing office, Washington, D.C. 20402.

Page 95: The Third Draft of the Proposed National Pastoral Letter of the U.S. Bishops on War and Peace, "The Challenge of Peace: God's Promise and Our Response," was published in *Origins*, NC Documentary Service, April 14, 1983.

Page 95: Lewis Thomas, noted biologist and essayist (*Lives of a Cell* and *The Medusa and the Snail*) is quoted from his article "Unacceptable Damage," which appeared in *The New York Review of Books*, September 24, 1981. Jonathan Schell has also discussed the idea that we have only one earth on page 76 of his book *The Fate of the Earth* (Avon, 1983).

CHAPTER EIGHT: The Way Out: The First Steps

Page 100: Dr Herbert York's quote is from his book *Race to Oblivion: A Participant's View of the Arms Race* (A Clarion Book, Simon & Schuster, 1970), page 230.

Pages 107–108: Admiral Gayler's proposal appeared in "How to Break the Momentum of the Nuclear Arms Race," in *The New York Times Magazine*, April 25, 1982.

CHAPTER NINE: Preventing Nuclear War Is Your Business

Page 120: Walter Cronkite is quoted in the brochure of the International Physicians for the Prevention of Nuclear War.

Page 120: Thomas J. Watson's quote is from "MX Isn't Issue No. 1," by Thomas J. Watson and Mark Garrison, *The New York Times*, January 26, 1983. Regarding business people speaking out, see "Are These Men Soviet Dupes?" by Florence Graves, *Common Cause*, January/February 1983.

Page 123: T. K. Jones is quoted in Chapter 2 of Robert Scheer's *With Enough Shovels* (Random House, 1982).